A Decade of Namibia

A Decade of Namibia

Politics, Economy and Society
The Era Pohamba, 2004–2015

By

Henning Melber

BRILL

LEIDEN | BOSTON

The chapters in this book on Namibia 2004–2014 were previously published in Brill's *Africa Yearbook. Politics, Economy and Society South of the Sahara 2004–2014*. The other chapters are published here for the first time.

Library of Congress Cataloging-in-Publication Data

Names: Melber, Henning, author.
Title: A decade of Namibia : politics, economy and society – the era Pohamba,
    2004–2015 / by Henning Melber.
Description: Leiden ; Boston : Brill, 2016. | Includes bibliographical
    references and index.
Identifiers: LCCN 2016014619 | ISBN 9789004319325 (pbk. : alk. paper)
Subjects: LCSH: Pohamba, Hifikepunye Lucas, 1935– | Namibia—Politics and
    government—21st century. | Namibia—Economic conditions—21st century. |
    Namibia—Social conditions—21st century.
Classification: LCC DT1649 .M445 2016 | DDC 968.81042—dc23 LC record available at http://lccn.loc.gov/2016014619

Want or need Open Access? Brill Open offers you the choice to make your research freely accessible online in exchange for a publication charge. Review your various options on brill.com/brill-open.

Typeface for the Latin, Greek, and Cyrillic scripts: "Brill". See and download: brill.com/brill-typeface.

ISBN 978-90-04-31932-5 (paperback)
ISBN 978-90-04-32157-1 (e-book)

Contents

Acknowledgements

This publication in the series "*A Decade of…*" is like the earlier two issues (featuring Mozambique and Ghana respectively) based on chapters previously published in the *Africa Yearbook. Politics, Economy and Society South of the Sahara*. It slightly deviates from the format due to an additional reference point: Hifikepunye Pohamba had been elected in 2004 as the second Head of State since Namibia's Independence and served two terms in office between March 2005 and March 2015. At the end of his presidency he was awarded the Mo Ibrahim Prize for good governance as the fifth statesman of the continent. This overview therefore covers – as the sub-title indicates – as a kind of 'long decade' the twelve years from his election in 2004 until his retirement, reviewing and documenting Namibia's development during his presidency. In addition, an introductory analysis precedes the chronological account, putting the Pohamba era into the overall context of Namibian society.

The author wishes to thank Joed Elich, Franca de Kort and Ellen Girmscheid of Brill for their continued support in this project during all the years and Peter Colenbrander and Carol Rowe for their meticulous language editing of the texts following.

The Era of President Pohamba and the Mo Ibrahim Prize

Namibia's first 25 years of national sovereignty were under the presidential governance of Sam Nujoma (1990–2005) and Hifikepunye Pohamba (2005–2015). This introductory overview contextualizes and assesses the era of the second Head of State, Hifikepunye Pohamba, who at the end of his terms was awarded the prestigious Mo Ibrahim Prize in recognition of the good governance attributed to his service in office. The chronology following this introductory essay is therefore documenting a "long decade". It starts in 2004, when in November Pohamba as presidential candidate of the South West Africa People's Organization (SWAPO), the former liberation movement and governing party since Independence, was elected by popular vote. It then covers his subsequent ten years in office from March 2005 to March 2015, and ends with the special ceremony when the Mo Ibrahim Prize was handed over to the then retired President on 20 November in Accra (Ghana). The two markers for the ten years in office therefore add up to twelve calendar years.

This Introduction links the Mo Ibrahim Prize with an assessment of the Namibian presidential democracy and the performance of President Pohamba. It thereby offers an analytical framework for the factual summary of the years 2004–2015 that follows and takes the liberty of commenting.[1] Although published in the series "*A Decade of…*", which compiles ten chapters originally published

---

1 Parts of this text are based on Henning Melber, "From Nujoma to Geingob: 25 Years of Presidential Democracy", *Journal of Namibian Studies*, no. 18, 2015, pp. 49–65.

in preceding volumes of the *Africa Yearbook*, this publication therefore slightly deviates from the standard format.[2]

The Mo Ibrahim Prize for Achievement in African Leadership

Established by the Sudanese telecommunication mogul Mo Ibrahim,
the Prize amounts to US$ 5,000,000 over ten years and US$ 200,000
annually for life thereafter. As the Mo Ibrahim Foundation declares,
the Prize, among other things, "showcases unsung heroes of the
African continent" and "recognizes African leaders who have dedi-
cated their tenure of office to developing their countries, improving
the welfare and livelihoods of their people and paving the way for
sustainable development".[3] Prize criteria also include the demonstration of exceptional leadership. When it was launched in 2007,
Nelson Mandela received the only Honorary Award so far, while
Mozambique's President Joaquim Chissano was awarded the first
regular Prize. Festus Mogae of Botswana was the recipient in 2008,
and Pedro Rodrigues of Cabo Verde in 2011. In 2009, 2010, 2012 and
2013 the Prize Committee concluded after its review that the Prize
would not be awarded. The Mo Ibrahim Foundation considers the
Prize as having

> the potential to change perceptions of African leadership by
> showcasing exceptional role models from the continent. The
> significance of the Prize lies not only with its winners but also
> with the conversation around leadership that it generates.[4]

---

2 See for previous editions Joseph Hanlon, *A Decade of Mozambique. Politics,
   Economy and Society 2004–2013*. Leiden and Boston: Brill 2015, and Michael
   Amoah, Kwesi Aning, Nancy Annan and Paul Nugent, *A Decade of Ghana.
   Politics, Economy and Society 2004–2013*. Leiden and Boston: Brill 2016.

3 http://www.moibrahimfoundation.org/prize/.

4 Ibid.

The leadership of Namibia's President Pohamba features at least indirectly (and partly directly) throughout the chronology of events of the years 2004 to 2015 compiled in this volume. His governance performance is also put into the general context of Namibia's presidential democracy in the parts to follow in this article. They critically reflect on the limits of the achievements as much as on the limited symbolic significance of the Mo Ibrahim Prize, which in the absence of better alternatives either remains unawarded or selects leaders of Pohamba's caliber.

The Presidentialization of Namibian Politics

Presidential politics has of late emerged as a new focus for scholarly debate, which seeks to explore further the impact and influence of presidents in democratic settings within a multi-party environment.[5] Such debate on what is also termed 'presidentialization' might find fertile ground in a Namibian case study. At the center of the interest is the impact and negotiating space presidents have or seek vis-à-vis the political party or parties and the utilization and application of the available space for maneuver.[6]

While Namibia has a presidential democracy, it is empirically to some extent a different case from most others in this category. Sam Nujoma, the first President of the Republic of Namibia, was elected prior to Independence by the members of the Constituent Assembly and sworn in on Independence Day, 21 March 1990. Since November 1994, every five years general elections for both the

---

5 See, for example, Gianluca Passarelli (ed.), *The Presidentialization of Political Parties. Organizations, Institutions and Leaders*. Basingstoke: Palgrave Macmillan 2015; Ludger Helms (ed.), *Comparative Political Leadership*. Basingstoke: Palgrave Macmillan 2012.

6 See Paul Chaisty, Nic Cheeseman and Timothy Power, "Rethinking the 'Presidentialism Debate': Conceptualizing Coalition Politics in Cross-Regional Perspective", *Democratization*, vol. 21, no. 1, 2014, pp. 72–94.

National Assembly and the President take place in separate but parallel votes. But at times one wonders whether the emphasis is on the presidency or on democracy, given the far-reaching powers vested in the office of the Head of State. He is backed by an overwhelming parliamentary majority, of which more than half are either Ministers or Deputy Ministers appointed by the same President – who may also dismiss them at any time. His authority as President, nominated by his party (the former liberation movement SWAPO), is even more widely anchored and accepted than the hegemony of the political organization he represents. Presidential election results have confirmed this: the party's presidential candidates garnered at every parallel election for parliament and president more votes than the party itself. Notably, the margin even increased markedly at the last elections.

Parliamentary and presidential election results for SWAPO 1994–2014

	1994	1999	2004	2009	2014
SWAPO	73.89%	76.15%	75.83%	75.27%	80.01%
Nujoma	74.46%	76.85%	–	–	–
Pohamba	–	–	76.44%	76.42%	–
Geingob	–	–	–	–	86.73%

As this shows, the three presidents elected by popular vote took office almost uncontested, despite several other parties and candidates seeking electoral support. Securing their position therefore depends less on the general electorate than on the inner-party constellation and support base. This is a contributory factor to making Namibia a case of "democratic authoritarianism", which stresses the hitherto decisive relevance of the hegemonic party, while at the same time confirming the extensive authority vested in the head of state as the party representative.[7]

The party's 2014 election campaign, under the motto "The Legacy Continues", depicted the three leaders with the sub-heading "Consolidating Peace, Stability, Prosperity", associating Nujoma with peace, Pohamba with stability and Geingob with prosperity. Such personification is more than a construct of spin-doctors. It resonates with the view of the majority of Namibians, who have a high degree of confidence and trust in the office holder. An Afrobarometer survey showed the following exceptional approval rates for trust and performance: Nujoma 76% and 78%, Pohamba 81% and 88%, and Geingob 79% and 89%.[8] Such votes of confidence represent considerable social capital, which can be applied in the exercise of office and underlines the presidential nature and focus of Namibian politics.

Namibia's Presidential Democracy

When the Constituent Assembly drafted the normative framework for the sovereign state to come, SWAPO advocated a strong presidential democracy. Members of other parties expressed preferences for a strong parliament and cabinet instead. Eventually, a compromise secured far-reaching powers for the President, but also some control function for the Parliament, based on the assumption that the latter's plural nature would allow for a certain watchdog role

---

7 Henning Melber, "Post-Liberation Democratic Authoritarianism: The Case of Namibia", *Politikon – South African Journal of Political Studies*, vol. 42, no. 1, 2015, pp. 45–66.

8 Institute for Public Policy Research/Afrobarometer, *News Release: Trust, Approval Ratings High for Namibia's President and Prime Minister Following a Long Trend*. Windhoek: Institute for Public Policy Research, 28 October 2014. The approval ratings for Nujoma were based on the results of a survey from 2002; Geingob's ratings were for his performance as prime minister.

vis-à-vis the President's party. Given SWAPO's hegemonic status, with a two-thirds majority in Parliament ever since the 1994 elections, this turned out to be more wishful thinking than political reality.

Evidence for this was the first constitutional change in 1998, when SWAPO, using its two-thirds majority in Parliament, modified the two-term limitation clause for State Presidents. The party created a "lex Nujoma": since Sam Nujoma was not directly elected by the people the first time round but appointed by the Constitutional Assembly, he was allowed to stand for re-election by popular vote for another (third) term. However, one has to concede that, with this exception, Namibian Presidents have so far been willing to hand over their power and retire.

The authority and competence of the Head of State is defined in chapter 5 of the Constitution (articles 27 ff.). Despite the existence of a Prime Minister, the President has ultimate charge over the Cabinet, whose members are appointed and dismissed at his/her sole personal discretion. He/she is in supreme command of the army and decides on appointments in all security organs and the Judicial Service Commission. The President can also single-handedly declare a state of emergency or war. Parliamentary control could in principle be exercised if a majority supported a motion of non-confidence in ministers, while the president, under article 57, can also dissolve Parliament, although this implies that new presidential elections would have to take place.

When comparing the Constitution with political reality, however, much depends on the composition of Parliament and the power of parties when it comes to the extent of a president's influence. After all, the President could also be ousted from office by a two-thirds majority in Parliament although, given the *de facto* one-party system prevailing, with SWAPO holding more than two-thirds of seats since 1995 with ever-increasing control so far over Parliament (amounting to 80% since 2015), this remains theory. Thus, the extent to which democratic rules are followed lies mainly at the discretion of the

President and the party. The only obstruction to the Head of State applying his/her power would come from within their own party's ranks. This seems a highly unrealistic prospect, since many of the Members of Parliament, who are supposed to control the Cabinet, are also appointed by the President as either Ministers or Deputy Ministers.[9] While they should exercise self-discipline, they normally take the floor in parliamentary debates as spokespersons of the party or the President, to whom they owe ultimate loyalty. Thus, the President of Namibia can claim a degree of almost unlimited omnipotence. The only factors of relevance are inner-party power relations and factions. Therefore, under the current constellation, the real election of a Head of State takes place within the party and, following a party decision in 2007, ultimately by the vote of the 400-plus delegates at the party congresses held every five years. These are the decisive moments, when the party president and the deputy president – and thereby the party's presidential candidate – are elected.

The Era Pohamba

While Nujoma was willing to leave the bridge of the Namibian ship, he was determined not to surrender the decision as to who should succeed him. His declared crown prince was his long-standing confidante Hifikepunye Pohamba. Born in 1935, he was, as SWAPO's Secretary for Finance, mainly in charge of the movement's infrastructure with respect to its civilian exile camps in Zambia and Angola and the main contact on the ground for those giving material support to the struggle. As an administrator respected for his

---

9 See Henning Melber, "People, Party, Politics and Parliament: Government and Governance in Namibia", in Mohamed Salih (ed.), *African Parliaments: Governance and Government*. Basingstoke: Palgrave Macmillan 2005 (also Cape Town: HSRC Press 2006), pp. 142–161.

integrity and loyalty, he had been a trusted low-key ally of Nujoma since the early "struggle days". Serving as a loyal minister with various portfolios since Independence, he made no noteworthy achievements during his terms in office.

Despite the blessing of the "old man", as Nujoma occasionally is fondly and respectfully called, a fierce battle over his succession took place. Upon initiative of Nujoma, Pohamba was appointed uncontested as the party's deputy president at the congress in August 2002. But only in 2004 did Nujoma finally confirm that he would definitely leave office at the end of his term. A subsequent extraordinary party congress had to elect a presidential candidate from among three contestants, and Nujoma's still decisive influence ensured that his preferred candidate was able to sail through, though the waters were choppier than anticipated.[10] The collateral damage included not only the dismissal of the main contender, Hidipo Hamutenya, from his office as Foreign Minister, but also a much wider McCarthy-like vendetta against all those suspected of not supporting the President's choice. The fall-out ultimately led to the founding of the new opposition party Rally for Democracy and Progress (RDP) by Hamutenya and like-minded individuals, including other long-serving high-ranking party officials from the first "struggle generation".[11]

---

10   See Henning Melber, "'Presidential Indispensability' in Namibia: Moving Out of Office but Staying in Power?", in Roger Southall and Henning Melber (eds), *Legacies of Power: Leadership Change and Former Presidents in African Politics*. Cape Town: HSRC Press und Uppsala: The Nordic Africa Institute 2006, pp. 98–119 (here: pp. 104–108).

11   The career of Hamutenya outside the party was, however, mixed and short-lived. While the RDP emerged as the official opposition in the parliamentary elections of 2009, it became almost irrelevant with the election results in 2014. Under pressure, Hamutenya surrendered the party presidency – and returned to the SWAPO family under Geingob's presi-

In contrast to the anticipated subservient role for him, Pohamba – reportedly originally reluctant to accept the new responsibility – managed to develop his own leadership style once in office. But, apart from being far less confrontational in nature than his predecessor, not much of it actually suggested any specific leadership qualities. Far more moderate and modest in tone and behaviour than his predecessor, Pohamba personified the humble servant of the people for most of his two terms in office, seeking to reconcile political rifts, including those caused over his nomination, and building bridges into other parts of the Namibian community. Guided by a strong Christian faith and, like his predecessor, rather conservative in his moral values and lifestyle, he had a "man of the people" appeal. In his personality, he had more of the features of a "father of the nation" than the more autocratic and patriarchal Nujoma. But Pohamba's kind of father figure soon showed wear and tear as a result of showing too much leniency and having too little stamina to bring about reform and fight corruption and graft, to which he had committed so prominently in his inaugural speech. Although the Anti-Corruption Commission was promptly established, spectacular misappropriation of public funds noticeably increased, while those prosecuted and punished were more the small fry than the big fish. While Pohamba's personal integrity was, despite some minor irritations, largely undisputed, he clearly disappointed those who had welcomed his promises not to compromise on fighting corruption.

Not least due to his reluctance to enter into conflicts, little spectacular happened during his decade in office. This was a source of both comfort and discomfort. The ambiguity of Pohamba's presidency was that too little too late (if anything at all) took place in terms of reforms, and that malpractices that had infiltrated the upper echelons of administration and politics were able to thrive still further. Pohamba's presidency was a vivid illustration that

dency in August 2015. Ahead of the Regional and Local Authorities elections in November 2015, he even publicly campaigned again for SWAPO.

popular rhetoric cannot replace implementation. The State of the
Nation Address (SONA) delivered in 2012 serves as a striking example. During the course of its delivery, Pohamba announced a Public
Finance Reform Programme and, as an integral part of it, the revi-
sion of Public Procurement Regulations. He promised that these
measures wold be "implemented without delay". He also affirmed
his "determination to fight corruption" and reiterated that this fight
"must be waged without fear or favour". He would therefore "direct
the Ministry of Justice to expedite the tabling of a strong and com-
prehensive legislation on the protection of whistle blowers". He
tasked the National Planning Commission to finalize without any
delay the National Human Resources Plan and ordered "that the
cleaning of public buildings and their surroundings be improved
without delay". Before ending, he stressed twice that words and
policies "must be turned into practical actions in order to make a
difference".[12]

Such suggestions of determination contrasted with the realities, and ultimately, in the absence of subsequent action, indicated
weakness rather than strength. The lack of leadership contrasting
with this SONA was bemoaned by the former editor of the popular
independent daily "The Namibian", who in her weekly column
suggested that "the former President should never have coerced
Pohamba into accepting the offer of the Presidency, because he has
been a reluctant participant from the outset". According to her, he
is a man,

> who to all intents and purposes, has good and decent attri-
> butes and the best of intentions (...) Had this been accompa-
> nied by a resolve to ensure he would not leave his office

---

12   Republic of Namibia, State of the Nation Address 2012 by His Excellency
      Hifikepunye Pohamba, President of the Republic of Namibia. Windhoek,
      25 April 2012, pp. 2, 4, 8, 9 and 13f., http://www.az.com.na/fileadmin/
      pdf/2012/az/State-of-the-Nation-04-26-12.pdf.

without having brought about some fundamental improvements in the lives of the people, President Pohamba would
most definitely have passed muster. As things stand right now,
he is the President who should never have been.[13]

The impression of a toothless tiger (or rather, in the African context, a clawless lion) was reinforced shortly afterwards, when it was
announced that 11 out of the 24 Permanent Secretaries were finally
re-shuffled on 1 June 2012, although the President had ordered this
move a year before. When massive mismanagement in the health
system and other sectors was discussed at a Cabinet meeting held
towards the end of May 2012, he lost his usual patience and com-
posure. He reportedly interrupted the debate and enquired, visibly enraged with Prime Minister Nahas Angula: "I wonder who is
in charge of the government if I gave instructions and a year later
we have to sit with the same problem that was not addressed".[14] As
rhetorical as the question was supposed to be, it would have been
unthinkable for it to have been asked by his predecessor – or should
be asked by his successor, for that matter.

But like them, he was occasionally not reluctant to use populist
rhetoric both before and during his terms as Head of State, especially
when deep-rooted mental affinities to the liberation struggle evoked
an authoritarian mind-set anchored in pseudo-radical anti-imperialist jargon. The tone of the congratulatory message conveyed to the
administrative secretary of ZANU-PF after Mugabe's fraudulent re-
election as Zimbabwe's President in 2002 speaks for itself. Signed by
Pohamba as the party's Secretary-General, it expressed

13   Gwen Lister, "Political perspective", *The Namibian*, 27 April 2012, http://
      allafrica.com/stories/201204270498.html.
14   Jan Poolman, "Reshuffle to 'stimulate' PSes", *The Namibian*, 30 May 2012,
      http://www.namibian.com.na/index.php?id=95639&page=archive-read.

on behalf of the leadership and the entire membership ... our elation over the resounding victory scored. ... Your party's triumph is indeed victory for Southern Africa in particular and the African continent at large. It is victory over neo-colonialism, imperialism and foreign sponsored puppetry. We in SWAPO Party knew quite well that despite imperialist intransigence and all round attempts by enemies of peace, democracy and the rule of law to influence the outcome of the elections in favour of neck-chained political stooges, people of Zimbabwe would not succumb an inch to external pressure. They spoke with one overwhelming voice to reject recolonization. Their verdict should, therefore, be respected unconditionally by both the external perpetrators of division and their hired local stooges, who have been parading themselves as democrats. ... As we join your great nation in celebrating this well deserved and indeed well earned victory over the forces of darkness and uncertainty, we wish to call upon the people of Zimbabwe to prove to the prophets of doom that they can do without their unholy blessing, through hard work. In the same vein, we call for unity of purpose among the African people as the only viable weapon to ward off outside influence.[15]

When he first took office, Pohamba did not use such martial language. In contrast to his predecessor, he was moderate and measured in his tone. But over his terms in office his frustration over

---

15   SWAPO Party/Office of the Secretary General, *Letter to ZANU/PF*, Windhoek, 14 March 2002. For the special relationship between Zimbabwe and Namibia, see Henning Melber, "In the Footsteps of Robert Gabriel Mugabe: Namibian Solidarity with Mugabe's Populism – Bogus Anti-imperialism in Practice", in Sabelo J. Ndlovu-Gathseni (ed.), *Mugabeism? History, Politics and Power in Zimbabwe*. London: Palgrave MacMillan 2015, pp. 107–120.

a lack of delivery seemed to affect his ability to remain low-key. During his last months as President, Pohamba displayed increasing signs of being an impatient and angry man, returning occasionally to similar rhetoric and contradicting his image as a father seeking to accommodate differences and diversities.

With regard to the unresolved land issue, he articulated increasingly strong views, as if he had not earlier also been responsible for land matters as a Minister. In an interview with Al Jazeera, Pohamba warned in October 2012:

> A conference on the land suggested that those who have plenty of land they should sell it to the government. And we tried to get the land from them, but unfortunately there is reluctance. Something else has to be tried. We are not talking about confiscation, we are talking about them to sell the land to the government in order for the government to distribute the land to – I don't like to use the word black – but to those who were formally disadvantaged by the situation.
>
> For the last 20 years we have been appealing to them, that please let's consider ourselves irrespective of our colour. As one people, as Namibians and if a Namibian is suffering, let's all sympathise with him. Here we have hundreds if not thousands of Namibian people who have no land and therefore are suffering. . . . We have the policy of willing seller, willing buyer, that has not been working for the last 22 years and I think something has to be done to amend the constitution so that the government is allowed to buy the land for the people. Otherwise, if we don't do that we will face a revolution. And if the revolution comes, the land will be taken over by the revolutionaries.[16]

---

16   Al Jazeera, "Pohamba: Namibia at the crossroads – Talk to Al Jazeera", 20 October 2012, http://www.aljazeera.com/programmes/talktojazeera/2012/10/20121012143428o992.html.

Ironically, Pohamba was, as Minister of Lands, Resettlement and Rehabilitation between 2000 and 2005, directly responsible for the painfully slow redistribution of land, when even funds allocated for the purchase of such land remained unutilized, and many offers to buy such farms were rejected. Far too little had happened during his tenure at the Ministry, before he took the oath as Head of State. The lack of results that he bemoaned was partly of his own making.

When confronted with critical responses from voters, who expressed frustration over the lack of delivery of improvements in the situation of ordinary people, he did not always behave as the gentleman he appeared to be most of the time. During a political rally in the region of Kavango West, disgruntled local residents threatened that they would not vote next time. In response, Pohamba suggested that they should then just stay at home.[17] In a similar fashion, during a presidential farewell tour through the country in December 2014, while inspecting the limited results of recent government initiatives, not least in housing and sanitation, Pohamba strongly criticised the lacklustre performance and lack of delivery. In the light of such re-positioning, a weekly newspaper close to the party published a scathing editorial, which, as a review of Pohamba's track record in office suggested:

> While one would like to sympathise with the outgoing president, who is so eager to leave a lasting legacy, whatever that is, one cannot help but feel that his anger is inconsequential and a little too late.
>
> This is a president who has been at the helm of the highest office in the land for ten years, and for him to start criss-crossing the country dishing out his wrath left, right and centre at

17   "Stay home if you do not want to vote – Pohamba", *The Namibian*, 16 December 2013, http://www.namibian.com.na/index.php?id=117735& page=archive-read.

> this moment in time when he is in the sunset of his presidency, sounds like a desperate cry for attention.
>
> (...) no one will take the outgoing president seriously when he starts screaming about lazy and incompetent officials when under his watch during the last ten years, a number of incompetent ministers kept their jobs. To some degree, incompetence has been the hallmark of his presidency. (...) The president cannot right the wrongs of his ten-year reign in just less than five months. (...) It is time for Pohamba to fade away.[18]

Pohamba never managed to obtain as much authority and omnipresence as his predecessor. Even when stepping out of his shadow, he secured hardly any visibility as a true leadership personality. While he occupied the moral high ground for most of his time in office, this never resulted in meaningful corrective measures. As it has been observed:

> Until recently, when he became more of a scold, his leadership style was more grandfatherly (moral leadership) than interventionist, activist. In such a scenario, the Cabinet becomes empowered (for good or otherwise), but bad behaviour also creeps in and corruption or incompetence becomes frozen and protected.[19]

---

18   "Our lame duck president", *Windhoek Observer*, 12 December 2014, http://observer24.com.na/editorial/3874-our-lame-duck-president.

19   Bill Lindeke, "Presidential Power and Performance in Namibia: The First Quarter Century", in *Celebrating 25 Years of Democratic Elections, 1989–2014.* Supplement of the Namibia Media Holdings on 23 December 2014 to the newspapers *Republikein*, *Namibian Sun* and *Allgemeine* Zeitung, p. 20.

President Pohamba: "One of the Unsung Heroes"?

Given these critical assessments, the Mo Ibrahim Foundation's announcement on 2 March 2015 that the outgoing Namibian Head of State was awarded the 2014 Ibrahim Prize for Achievement in African Leadership was rather unexpected. The Prize Committee justified the decision to give the fourth Award to Pohamba by saluting

> his role in maintaining and consolidating his country's stability and prosperity and for forging national cohesion and reconciliation at a key stage of Namibia's consolidation of democracy and social and economic development. The Prize also recognizes his contribution in cementing Namibia's reputation as a well-governed, stable and inclusive democracy with strong media freedom and respect for human rights.[20]

During the special ceremony in Accra on 20 November, when the Prize was handed over to Pohamba, Salim Ahmed Salim, as the chair of the independent Prize Committee, added: "His ability to command the confidence and the trust of his people is exemplary."[21] And Mo Ibrahim declared on the same occasion:

> We need to change the narrative about African leadership. The world knows everything about our bad leaders, but nothing about our heroes, especially those who are doing wonderful things for their people. We need role models – we need

---

20   http://www.moibrahimfoundation.org/prize/laureates/hifikepunye-pohamba/.

21   "President Hifikepunye Pohamba accepts Ibrahim Prize for Achievement in African Leadership", Press Release by the Mo Ibrahim Foundation, 20 November 2015, http://static.moibrahimfoundation .org/u/2015/11/20220344/Pohamba-press-release.pdf.

heroes – to inspire and motivate our young people. President Pohamba is one of the unsung heroes of Africa.[22]

In his acceptance speech, Pohamba concluded that,

the new African leader must strive to deliver peace, unity and equitable development. This means governing in the best interest of all citizens, regardless of the political, ethnic or religious affiliation of communities. It also underscores the importance of full compliance with constitutional provisions for presidential term limits.

Africa will be better positioned to achieve our collective ideals for peace and stability, development and progress when leaders commit to prioritising the interest of the people and do everything in their power to achieve these goals while they have the mandate of leadership.[23]

Let us for a moment compare the rationale for awarding this Prize to the retired Namibian Head of State with some of the markers during his terms in office (also featuring in the events presented in the chronological records that follow). Namibia has indeed remained a country of relative peace and stability and compares favorably in its democratic and human rights record with most other countries on the continent. With SWAPO taking some 80% of votes in the last parliamentary elections, however, one starts wondering how democratic Namibia's democracy really can be in the absence of any level playing field. This creates tempting opportunities to misunderstand the rule of law as the law of the rulers.

An example of this during the Pohamba era was the change from the election of governors in the country's regions by elected members of the regional council to their appointment by the Head

---

22   Ibid.

23   Ibid.

of State. When this was introduced by law in October 2010,[24] it set aside the constitutional clauses that gave such powers to the elected members of the regional councils as defined in articles 108 and 109. Pohamba also decided in December 2012, in violation of the constitutional definition of the composition of Cabinet (article 35), that the newly elected Secretary-General of SWAPO would become an *ex officio* member of Cabinet.[25] Pohamba also used his office to arrange in November 2012 a fundraising dinner at State House, at the taxpayer's expense, to secure donations for the forthcoming SWAPO Congress. Some twenty members of the business community reportedly paid N$ 100,000 each for a seat at the President's table.[26]

But the democratic culture and the maintenance of law also showed serious flaws in more fundamental aspects. During the Pohamba administration, a high treason trial took place of, originally, more than 120 people arrested in 1999 on a charge of planning and instigating a failed secessionist attempt in the North Eastern Caprivi region of the country. They had remained in prison without a verdict being reached. At the end of 2015, barely a quarter of them were found guilty and sentenced, while more than twenty of those held had already died in prison.[27] Most of the accused who were

---

24   Regional Governor's Appointment Amendment Act, No. 20 of 2010; submitted to Parliament, having been moved by the then Minister of Trade and Industry Hage Geingob (since then Prime Minister and as from 2015 Namibia's President) with the argument that this would enhance direct democracy.

25   Catherine Sasman, "Mbumba's presence in Cabinet under Spotlight", *The Namibian*, 22 March 2013, http://www.namibian.com.na/index .php?id=106483&page=archive-read.

26   Shinovene Immanuel, "N$ 100k dinner raises eyebrows", *The Namibian*, 12 November 2012, http://www.namibian.com.na/index.php?id=102241& page=archive-read.

27   For a background analysis, see Henning Melber, "One Namibia, One Nation? The Caprivi as a Contested Territory", *Journal of Contemporary African Studies*, vol. 27, no. 4, 2009, pp. 463–481.

still alive were finally released after more than 15 years imprison-
ment without being found guilty of any of the charges. According
to article 12 1(b) of the Constitution a trial "shall take place within a
reasonable time, failing which the accused shall be released". With
regard to the much praised political freedoms, it is at least worth
noting, too, that the United Democratic Party (UDP), which advo-
cates for more autonomy for the Northeastern region formerly
called the Caprivi strip (now Zambezi) but distances itself from any
violence, had been declared illegal and all related political activities
banned since September 2006.[28]

On the economic front, the track record was similarly disput-
able. The biggest investment programs implemented during the
Pohamba administration failed to achieve the planned results.
A Targeted Intervention Program for Employment and Economic
Growth had allocated N$ 9.1 billion over three financial years
(N$ 14.7 billion including public works programs) as from 2011/12
for employment creation, but failed to create the targeted number
of jobs in the economy. The other major initiative was a low-cost
housing project on a grand scale. Introduced in 2013, the project was
allocated N$ 2.9 billion in 2013. The creation of modest but more
or less decent housing for tens of thousands of people was supposed to be the lasting legacy of Pohamba's presidency. The project
failed utterly and had already been shelved in 2014 due to a lack of
implementation.[29] In 2015 it was abandoned completely and ended
as a financial disaster for the public purse – though not for some

---

28   "Namibia. Caprivi political party declared illegal", *IRIN News*, 11 September
      2006, http://www.irinnews.org/report/60892/namibia-caprivi-political-
      party-declared-illegal.

29   By then, 25 local companies had received tenders. Of these, eight had
      been established only three years before, twelve during the previous
      two years, three had only been in the business for one year, and one was
      established only in 2014. None of the companies had the experiences
      stipulated in the tender. See Shinovene Immanuel and Tileni Mongudhi,

beneficiaries.[30] Rather, it created new temptations for so-called tenderpreneurs to enrich themselves as middlemen and -women by obtaining tenders that they had no competence to implement on their own.[31]

Meanwhile, the retirement mansion constructed for President Pohamba was estimated to have cost at least N\$ 35 million:

> Media reports indicate that the ground floor of Pohamba's mansion includes four garages, three guest rooms, and a dining area for 30 persons, a main guest lounge, as well as a private lounge, kitchen and laundry room, bar and braai area, a double volume lobby, a library and an office.
>
> The top floor will have three family bedrooms, accommodation for staff, another two bedrooms, a family lounge, gym and a helicopter landing space. (…)
>
> Presidential Affairs Minister Albert Kawana has in the past explained that the arrangement of making available residences for outgoing presidents is aimed to accord the 'neces-

---

"Mass housing put on ice", *The Namibian*, 21 May 2014, http://www.namibian.com.na/index.php?id=123524&page=archive-read.

30   Among these were most notably also his then 26-year-old daughter Kaupumhote Pohamba, a graduate in information technology from the Polytechnic of Namibia. Together with the daughter of an influential financial manager, she runs Kata Investments. The company was only established in 2013 but has obtained since then several tenders for public works including water supply and road construction and was also successful in bidding for the housing programme. Since then, public media have critically reported on some of the deals. See i.a. Shinovene Immanuel and Thileni Mongudi, "Pohamba's daughter chases N\$638m", *The Namibian*, 17 November 2014, http://www.namibian.com.na/index.php?page=archive-read&id=130613.

31   Shinovene Immanuel, "New mass housing prices – tenderpreneurs enjoy lavish spree", *The Namibian*, 27 June 2014, http://www.namibian.com.na/index.php?id=124968&page=archive-read.

sary respect to our leaders and it will benefit the peace and stability in the country'. (...)

The Former Presidents' Pension and Other Benefits Act outlines several benefits for former Presidents, from pension, benefits of the spouse, dependants, insolvency, exemption from income tax, residential home and offices.

According to that Act, Pohamba will be paid a monthly pension equal or greater than the monthly basic salary that he received immediately before leaving office as President or 80% of his successor's salary.

Pohamba will leave with at least 10 security personnel, unless the number is increased by Cabinet. He will have three drivers, two private secretaries, two personal assistants and two office attendants.

At his new home, Pohamba will be entitled to three domestic workers, two gardeners, two cooks, two waiters and two laundry workers. He will also be given three vehicles while his entertainment allowance and other costs will be determined by Cabinet.[32]

One does not need to blame the President personally for such benefits being bestowed upon him. Nor is he alone responsible for the failure of the most prestigious government induced initiatives to promote the wellbeing of ordinary citizens. One should also not imply that the Head of State deliberately and willfully supported his daughter's meteoric ascendancy into the black empowerment business world without any obvious qualifications except her name, dubious as this career is at least in moral and ethical terms. But it left a bitter taste and provoked public fury when it was disclosed by some investigative local journalism that another of Pohamba's

---

32   Shinovene Immanuel, "Pohamba mansion worth 100 low-cost-houses", *The Namibian*, 1 October 2014, http://www.namibian.com.na/index .php?id=128631&page=archive-read.

daughters was a beneficiary of a stipend scheme secretly offered by the Chinese government to nine Namibian students from privileged (politically highly influential) families for studies in the People's Republic, while thousands of young Namibians have no financial means to translate the educational qualifications obtained under much harsher conditions into an opportunity for academic study. This even became a newsworthy item in established US media.[33]

Taking stock and leaving aside the personal aspects of accepting privileges that come with the office for him and his family, President Pohamba's track record was at best mixed. Admittedly, he did not do much harm and Namibia's relative political stability prevailed. But delivery in terms of measurable results of good governance remained modest at best. As the figures compiled annually by the United Nations Development Program in its Human Development Report document, Namibia remains among the countries with the highest income discrepancy in the world. While it ranges as a higher middle-income country with an average annual per capita income of US$ 9,400 in 2015, undisputed estimates of the Food and Agriculture Organization of the United Nations released in mid-2015 classified more than 42% of the country's population as malnourished. This prompted a commentator in the state-owned daily newspaper to observe:

> There comes a time in the life of any nation when silence is no longer golden and when there is a fine line between silence and betrayal. That time has descended upon us as a nation to address our challenges with equanimity. These challenges

---

33   Sharon LaFraniere, "China helps the powerful in Namibia", *The New York Times*, 19 November 2009, http://www.nytimes.com/2009/11/20/world/asia/20namibia.html?_r=0.

include, among others, the grinding poverty, degradation and destitution facing the majority of Namibians.[34]

With the award of the Mo Ibrahim Prize, Pohamba left office on a high note, praised by a proud Namibian public for such an achievement. But a much more somber conclusion seems justified:

> As Africa's fourth Ibrahim Prize laureate retires ... his moderation should be regarded as a two-edged sword. Namibia is marginally more free today than it was ten years ago, with political dissent more readily tolerated, minorities less frequently demonised, government pressure on independent media outlets diminished, and intra-SWAPO squabbles more skillfully resolved. But Pohamba's caution, conservatism, and lack of dynamism have also combined to ensure that President Geingob faces almost as many developmental challenges in 2015 as his predecessor did in 2005.[35]

As several more of the data and events summarized in the following chronology for the years 2004 to 2015 document, recognizing President Pohamba as an "unsung hero" seems to cast doubts on the standards that qualify individuals to be awarded a highly remunerated Prize for Achievement in African Leadership. If the Pohamba era is the best African leadership performance can offer, then the Prize is a reward for those who do not deliberately abuse their power and at least have the decency to try to live up to the oath of office they took. Not less, but definitely also not more.

---

34   Charles Mubita, "Silently starving and malnourished in peace", *New Era*, 24 July 2015, https://www.newera.com.na/2015/07/24/silently-starving-malnourished-peace/.

35   Ian Cooper, "Namibia and President Pohamba's Legacy." Guest post at *Presidential Power. Presidents and Presidential Politics Around the World.* Posted on 26 March 2015 at http://presidential-power.com/?p=3053.

Namibia in 2004

As a result of the parliamentary, presidential and regional elections, the South West African Peoples' Organisation (SWAPO) of Namibia further consolidated its dominance. The nomination of SWAPO's presidential candidate – succeeding the country's first head of state and president of the former liberation movement since its foundation in 1960 – resulted in fierce intra-party competition and the sidelining of longstanding political office bearers. The land issue became further politicised and initiatives to expropriate land contributed to growing insecurity among commercial farmers. Overall macroeconomic performance suffered through export losses due to the strong currency. Public expenditure came under pressure as debts accumulated further, and state finances face a critical degree of constraint.

Domestic Politics

The biggest shifts in the domestic political power structure – maybe since independence in 1990 – took place as a prelude to this year's parliamentary and presidential elections. Due to internal party opposition, Namibia's head of state Sam Nujoma – along with Robert Mugabe, the only remaining independence-era president still in office – decided against pursuing a fourth term. He suggested Hifikepunye Pohamba, the party's vice-president and his closest confidante, to the central committee as his successor. The committee met on 2 and 3 April to prepare submissions to an extraordinary SWAPO congress on the *presidential candidate*, but denied Pohamba the status of sole candidate and nominated three potential successors. Delegates to the extraordinary SWAPO congress, held from 28 to 30 May, were tasked with making a final choice. During the internal campaign, the factional fights revealed disunity to an extent hitherto unseen.

Nujoma used his executive powers as head of state to *dismiss Foreign Minister* Hidipo Hamutenya, Pohamba's strongest contender and rival, from his cabinet post on 25 May, just ahead of the congress. Hamutenya's deputy, Kaire Mbuende (former SADC executive secretary), considered a supporter of his minister, also had to vacate office with immediate effect. Notwithstanding such drastic harassment, almost one-third of the more than 500 congress delegates voted for Hamutenya in the first round, which, however, failed to produce a candidate with an absolute majority. Snatching all but one vote from the third candidate, Nahas Angula, minister of higher education and employment creation (allegedly a "fall-back candidate" for Nujoma in case his favourite did not make it), Pohamba finally emerged as clear winner.

The result of the subsequent *electoral convention* held by the party's central committee from 1 to 3 October was the rigorous implementation of the Nujoma line and the strict exclusion of the so-called Hamutenya camp from the party's medium-term political future. The number of votes candidates received decided their ranking on the party list, which was headed by 12 candidates nominated by the president. The party held 55 of 72 parliamentary seats, having won 75% of all votes in the 1999 elections. Hamutenya ended in the 57th position – an obvious indication that he would be prevented from returning as a legislator and cabinet member (ministers have to be members of parliament). The same fate befell those considered to be his supporters, including several ministers as well as the speaker of parliament. They were ranked even lower on the list. The minister of agriculture, another of the victims, drew his own conclusions and tendered his resignation on 7 December. Seemingly with the blessing of Nujoma, former Prime Minister Hage Geingob made his return to Namibian politics. Ousted from office by the president halfway through the third legislature, Geingob had joined a World Bank agency for Africa in Washington DC. He attended the convention, made himself available as a candidate and was ranked sufficiently favourably to ensure safe re-election as a member of the next parliament.

The *parliamentary and presidential elections* on 15 and 16 November were initially beset by minor organisational flaws, mainly in remote rural areas, due to computer problems and the weather conditions. According to all observer missions, the voting process was free and fair. Of a record number of 838,447 ballots (some 85% of close to one million registered voters), SWAPO again secured more than 75% of the valid votes and 55 of the 72 seats in the *National Assembly* with effect from March 2005. In the fourth parliament, parliamentarians will represent seven different parties (previously five), with six of them sharing 17 seats.

Opposition parties were more divided than ever before both internally and among themselves, while the different party platforms represented few if any substantive policy alternatives. The Congress of Democrats (CoD) maintained its second rank in the party political landscape, despite a decline from seven to five seats. Its members had been partly recruited from the ranks of dissenting SWAPO activists prior to the parliamentary elections in 1999. The Democratic Turnhalle Alliance (DTA), the official opposition at independence, has been in steady decline and retained four of its previous seven seats. The Herero-based National Unity Democratic Organisation (NUDO) separated from the ranks of the DTA and obtained three seats of its own. The United Democratic Front (UDF) – another ethnically oriented interest group, rooted in the Damara communities – consolidated its position by increasing its seats from two to three. Like NUDO, the Republican Party (RP), supported mainly by members of the white minority, campaigned for the first time outside the DTA and gained one seat. Surprisingly, the Monitor Action Group (MAG), representing the most conservative white element in postcolonial Namibia, managed to keep its one seat.

Voters expressed unexpectedly high confidence in SWAPO's new *presidential candidate*, Hifikepunye Pohamba, who was elected in parallel through separate ballot papers. Like his predecessor, he obtained more votes than the party (76.4%). Given the preceding conflict around his nomination, this was a surprising victory and an impressive sign of party unity, despite internal differences. As Nujoma remains in office as SWAPO president until the next ordinary party congress in 2007, close collaboration between the comrades of almost fifty years and continuity in SWAPO politics (and, hence, Namibian politics) seems likely.

Numerous minor irregularities and inconsistencies in electoral procedures, however, provoked *legal intervention* by the CoD and RP. They filed a court case to be able to view documents the Electoral Commission of Namibia (ECN) had refused to disclose. The high court ruled on 16 December in favour of the application. On the basis of the evidence collected, CoD and RP contested the election results in the high court on 21 December. They claimed they had discovered an array of failures to comply with the Electoral Act, and discrepancies between voting figures and results, as well as a series of other irregularities. The court was expected to pass judgment in early February 2005.

Regional elections took place on 29 and 30 November and SWAPO enjoyed another landslide victory, thereby confirming its overwhelming dominance. The turnout of more than half (53.5%) of the almost one million registered voters was markedly lower than in the national elections. The party garnered 96 of the 107 constituencies and increased its seats in the 13 regional councils (which also appoint the members to the National Council) from 80% to 90%. Another series of intrigues and power struggles accompanied the nomination of the party's candidates. The most prominent victim was the previous chairperson of the National Council, whose career came to an end.

The *local authority elections* held on 14 May were already characterised by local feuds in numerous urban centres, as party members plotted over the candidate list. Party headquarters interfered in several cases, imposing its own views and even appointed councillors other than those elected. Protests in a variety of municipal constituencies revealed anything but unity on the ground. This tempted President Nujoma to use election rallies on 8 and 9 May to warn against the invasive forces of imperialism and capitalism, forces that would divide even SWAPO's leadership. All told, the various elections during the year consolidated SWAPO's hegemony, but also exposed a degree of internal tension and division hitherto unseen.

Anti-imperialist rhetoric was also deployed in mid-June by government spokespersons to dismiss critical references in Amnesty International's (AI) annual report for 2003 on *human rights* in Namibia. The report was criticised as the "usual garbage", lacking in substance. AI had expressed concern about arbitrary detentions and excessive use of force by police and special units, and about undue delay in the *Caprivi high treason trial*. The latter had dragged on since the failed secessionist plot in August 1999, in the aftermath of which more than 120 suspects were arrested and continue to be held in custody. The trial only started during 2003, and numerous technicalities and legal disputes have since prolonged the deliberations, and there is no end in sight. In the meantime, more of the arrested suspects have died than people were killed during the original skirmishes.

The year 2004 brought reminders of one of the darkest chapters in the country's *colonial history*. However, no senior government official attended the ceremonies, which marked the hundredth anniversary of the beginning of the Herero war against German colonial occupation on 11 January 1904. This conflict resulted in what is considered to be the first genocide of the 20th century. The government commemorated the centenary by issuing a special stamp on the theme of reconciliation on 21 March (Independence Day). Nujoma's designated successor as head of state, however, did attend the ceremony, in which a German minister also participated (see below).

Foreign Affairs

In his new year's message, the president pledged that Namibia would continue to pursue what he termed "*principles of economic diplomacy*" as the core of its foreign policy. The country's international engagement was indeed largely confined to trade and economic negotiations and agreements. The good relations with East Asian countries continued to feature prominently. These operate with companies and contractors in Namibia and employ their own citizens in large-scale projects – much to the dismay of local stakeholders, such as industry and trade unions. *China* honoured Nujoma with the publication of a Chinese version of his autobiography, handed to him on 20 July on occasion of his 12th visit. The Chinese-Namibian trade volume increased by 52% between 2002 and 2003 to reach almost $ 75 m. It was announced during his visit that the five members of the Southern African Customs Union (SACU) would negotiate a free trade agreement with China. Nujoma then travelled to *Malaysia*. Several thousand workers are employed in a textile factory in Windhoek established by a Malaysian company under the AGOA and with considerable material support from Namibian authorities. This project is considered a success by both governments, notwithstanding massive criticism of environmental damage, appalling employment conditions and numerous violations of labour standards and practices, including the illegal employment of several hundred unqualified contract workers from Bangladesh, a scandal that made local headlines during September.

The Asian trip was part of a round of farewell visits by the president. He had already underlined the good relations to *Brazil* by meeting President Lula da Silva on 21 June, mainly to discuss trade matters and defence cooperation. Brazil seeks to strike a deal worth $ 35 m for supplying ships to the nascent Namibian navy. Nujoma also met President Castro while visiting *Cuba* from 22 to 24 June. Between his overseas journeys, and in connection with them, he stopped in several *African countries* (Zambia, Ghana, Kenya,

Tanzania, Angola) and attended the summit of the AU in Addis Ababa on 8 July. President Chissano from Mozambique, was in Windhoek on 6 and 7 December on his own farewell visit.

Due to the dismissal of both the minister of foreign affairs and his deputy in May (see above), Namibia's international policy was hardly visible except for the president's activities. The new foreign minister had no track record in diplomatic affairs and displayed no ambitions in this regard before the end of the legislative session. In the campaign to marginalise those considered to be in the Hamutenya camp, five officials previously nominated for postings abroad were instructed in December that their appointments had been revoked. The minister of trade and industry, originally supposed to sign a trade agreement with Mercosur ('Mercado Comœn del Cono Sur') in Brazil on behalf of a SACU delegation in mid-December, was replaced without notice upon Nujoma's intervention by the minister of fisheries. The Brazilian government told the trade and industry minister upon his arrival that he was no longer expected and had no role to play.

A century after the *colonial genocide*, the government agreed with the official German position. This is that no apology will be offered, which might have implications for compensation claims being pursued by a group of Herero in a US court. Chancellor Gerhard Schröder, during his first visit to African countries at the end of January, did not include the former colony in his travel plans. However, the German minister for economic cooperation and development attended the commemoration of the battle at Ohamakari near the Waterberg on 11 August. She acknowledged the German warfare as genocide from a modern perspective. Asked for an apology (the word did not appear in the text she read), she explained that her whole statement was an apology. There was, however, no visible change of policy on the issue of compensation for particular groups. If, how, and to what extent the descendants of the victims (mainly Herero and Nama) will be compensated for the historical injustices and their consequences remains to be seen. During her visit on 19 November, the parliamentary secretary of state at the German ministry for economic cooperation and development indicated that Germany would increase its financial support for the redistribution of land. Germany is Namibia's biggest single donor country. Namibians receive more German development funds per capita than anyone else.

Zimbabwe's minister of information, Jonathan Moyo, commented on the land issue (see more below) during an official five-day visit in the last week of February. He expressed satisfaction with the historical moment he could attend when government expressed its determination to pursue expropriation of land from commercial farmers, but dismissed speculation that there was anything more than coincidence between his presence and the announcement. Shortly after, and following the signing of a memorandum of understanding by the two governments, a team of six *experts from Zimbabwe* assisted Namibian authorities with advice in the area of land evaluation and surveying. Minister Moyo's visit served to establish a common *newspaper for the Southern African region* published jointly by the two governments, on the basis of a memorandum of understanding signed with his Namibian counterpart. The two information ministers launched the first issue of 'The Southern Times' on 3 September at Victoria Falls. A further plan foresees the establishment of a 24-hour satellite television news channel, Africa World, to be set up through a joint venture involving the two state broadcasting companies.

These *close Namibian-Zimbabwean ties* were further underlined by President Nujoma in his opening speech at Zimbabwe's international trade fair in Bulawayo on 29 April, during which he stressed that Namibia supported Zimbabwe "openly, whether imperialists like it or not." He assured his hosts at a banquet that Namibia would, in the event of an attack, send its army to the rescue within 24 hours and praised the president and people of Zimbabwe for being "a shining example of resisting imperialism and colonialism."

Socioeconomic Developments

The country's new president-elect served during 2004 as minister of lands, resettlement and rehabilitation. He signalled his hitherto unsuspected determination to pursue an increasingly proactive *land policy*. In a televised statement on 25 February, Prime Minister Theo Ben Gurirab announced that government would, in addition to its policy of willing seller-willing buyer, now also expropriate land within the constitutionally defined framework. He said more than 240,000 people were registered and waiting to be resettled. Minister Pohamba confirmed in parliament on 2 March the intention to implement land redistribution more aggressively. In his May Day speech, President Nujoma emphasised that *expropriation of farms* would not only target under-utilised land, but also serve as a punitive measure. He warned "minority racist farmers" that "steps will be taken and we can drive them out of this land ... as an answer to the insult to my Government."

A letter of 10 May by Pohamba was sent to some 15 farmers expressing "interest in acquiring their property." In response, a minority of white farmers embarked on a confrontational course. At a meeting on 9 June, they polarised the issue by expressing open defiance of government policy and accusing the commercial farmers' Namibia Agricultural Union (NAU) of pursuing a sell-out strategy. This drew strong reactions from the trade unions and SWAPO representatives. By mid-year the land issue was being widely canvassed in public debate. This matter was also reported and commented on, mainly critically in the international (particularly German) media, which often drew (so far largely unfounded) parallels with Zimbabwe.

The initial provisional valuation role for the 12,509 registered commercial farms in the country, mainly owned by around 3,800 white farmers, was closed on 29 September, after a month for inspection. This was a clear step towards implementing the long-announced plans to introduce a *land tax*, which aims to raise some

N$ 20 m annually. At the end of October, Minister Pohamba stated that government had since independence purchased 137 farms, totalling close to 875,000 hectares, on which over 1,500 families had been resettled.

Finance Minister Saara Kuugongelwa-Amadhila tabled the *annual budget for 2004/2005* on 24 March in parliament. Considered to be conservative and typical for an election year, government spending was projected to increase by 3.6% to N$ 12.7 bn. The budget deficit, at N$ 589 m, was estimated to be 1.6% of Namibia's GDP and supposedly well below the 3% target government had earlier set (but failed to meet in most years). The finance minister repeated appeals for *fiscal discipline* from previous years. Government debt by the end of the fiscal year (31 March) had reached 30.3% and was projected to reach 32% a year later. National debts had ballooned by 30% from N$ 7.9 to 10.2 bn between the 2002/3 and 2003/4 financial years. As the budget allocations revealed, government now spends approximately the same proportion of the budget (about 9%) on each of defence, public order, health and debt servicing.

An *analysis of the past 15 budgets* by the local Institute for Public Policy Research (IPPR) in July, saw "little reason to believe that public spending is becoming more equitable and more focused on the poor", but found evidence of "a strong suspicion that public spending is increasingly being channelled to more privileged groups in society employed in activities that bring little in the way of returns through higher economic growth, such as in defence, paramilitary security, intelligence and poorly performing parastatals." It concluded that "it is quite possible that poverty and inequality have worsened and that the national budget has done little to offset this trend."

Several factors contributed to *negative economic performance*. Fisheries suffered from the high exchange rate and a low fishing quota. The industry was additionally hampered by labour unrest and strikes. The chamber of mines recorded positive new developments and investments in the mining sector, but also myriad problems. Government finance suffered from a lack of taxes not only as a result of sluggish economic performance but also due to decreased revenue from a revised SACU agreement. Some N\$ 270 m less income was anticipated, increasing the budget deficit to 2.7%. As a result, and in combination with the growing debt services, the finance minister announced in parliament on 1 December that for the first time there will be no *additional budget*. Instead, the remaining N\$ 148 m in *contingency funds* were distributed without parliamentary approval on a variety of items, none of which (except one previously released disbursement to support flood victims in the Caprivi) qualified as unexpected expenditure. Among the biggest payments was an advance to meet contractual obligations in the building of the new state house (N\$ 52 m). This is a controversial monument, constructed – like Heroes' Acre a few years earlier – by North Korean contractors. Its costs are now estimated to exceed N\$ 750 m.

Against the background of these sobering realities, the country's long-term national development policy, *Vision 2030*, was officially launched on 2 June – six years after President Nujoma had initiated the blueprint. Complementing and guiding the five-yearly national development plans, Vision 2030 aims to place the quality of life of all Namibians on a par with people in the developed world by 2030. It assumes that by then the country will have a population of no less than three million people (currently below two million) and an unemployment rate of less than 5% of the work force (currently estimated between 30% to 40%, depending on the criteria).

On 1 July, the *World Bank* approved a Global Environment Facility (GEF) grant of \$ 7.1 m. This signals a deviation from the government's previous refusal to deal with international financial institutions. During the year, Namibia's ranking in the Human Development Index (HDI) dropped by 2 positions and the ILO report presented at the Bangkok AIDS conference on 14 July estimated that more than

150,000 people among the country's labour force were HIV positive. It further projected that *life expectancy* (in previous years well above 60 years) had been reduced to 44 years. Fifteen years after independence, the average lifespan of the Namibian people had dropped below the level prior to decolonisation.

Namibia in 2005

Fifteen years after independence, the country witnessed the first change at the top of its government, but the retiring head of state remained leader of the party in power. Hence, during the year speculation continued as to who was really exercising decisive political control. Intra-party factionalism continued unabated as a result of the contested leadership. While the new state president announced that a campaign of zero tolerance towards corruption would be a cornerstone of his term in office, the country was rocked by the biggest financial scandals to date.

Domestic Politics

The year began with a hangover from the earlier overwhelming electoral success of the former liberation movement SWAPO, which won a majority of three-quarters in both the parliamentary and presidential elections of November 2004. Opposition parties initiated *legal action to contest the parliamentary election results.* The Congress of Democrats (CoD), the biggest opposition party, and the Republican Party (RP) were the original complainants but were joined in the court case in mid-January by another three parties. They challenged the Electoral Commission of Namibia (ECN) over a series of observed irregularities and questioned the final election results published in the government gazette of 3 January. On 10 March, the high court ordered a vote recount. This took place under reportedly hectic and chaotic circumstances in order to meet the deadline for swearing in the new parliament and president before independence day (21 March). On 16 March, the ECN announced the outcome of the recount, which resulted in only minor differences from the original results, thus leaving the distribution of parliamentary seats unchanged. The two main complainants

© KONINKLIJKE BRILL NV, LEIDEN, 2016 | DOI 10.1163/9789004321571_004

questioned the recount procedures and registered their objections to the influence of SWAPO officials in the process. However, they did not appeal in court. The 72 newly elected members of the (4th) National Assembly (55 of them SWAPO) were subsequently sworn in on 20 March.

Speculation as to whether outgoing President Nujoma would indeed retire created an atmosphere of growing fear. Rumours warned of a plot to assassinate Pohamba in order to keep Nujoma in office for emergency reasons. Additional security measures to protect the designated president were implemented in early March. Finally, Hifikepunye Pohamba took the official oath as the *new head of state* during the orderly ceremonies on independence day. In the presence of several (mainly Southern) African heads of state, he announced in his inauguration speech his 'zero tolerance' campaign against corruption and the growing abuse of public funds.

A minor surprise was the appointment of Nahas Angula as the new prime minister. He had been one of the two other contenders to succeed Nujoma, but had then sided with Pohamba against the third aspirant, Hidipo Hamutenya. The *new cabinet* reflected a blend of the old guard and some 'young turks' (mainly as deputy ministers). These appointees had enjoyed the favour of Nujoma for being among his staunchest supporters. Their presence in government deliberately signalled continuity according to the will of the retired president. However, a few of the other appointments reflected his successor's desire to heal some of the wounds in the party caused by the disputed succession issue. All told, the new team provided few surprises.

Pohamba's *autonomy as head of state* was limited by the fact that the former state president would remain as the SWAPO party president (which he had been since the founding of the movement in 1960) until the next congress in 2007. Consequently, the question as to who exerted real power over policy matters, including state affairs, remained a prominent and contested issue and the rifts within SWAPO did not diminish, despite Pohamba's conciliatory efforts. Instead, new conflicts emerged between the old president and his chosen successor.

The limited room for manoeuvre was illustrated in the obstacles to the uncompromising pursuit of the *anti-corruption campaign* when party influence was strong. Pohamba reiterated his commitment to the fight against corruption in a speech at a rally on 'Cassinga day', commemorating the massacre by South African troops in a SWAPO refugee camp in Southern Angola (4 May). He stated that greed had become akin to colonialism and issued a stern warning to all who placed self-enrichment above the public interest. Corruption, tribalism and nepotism would not be tolerated. A week later, the deputy director in the office of the auditor-general declared at a public meeting in his private capacity that a lack of accountability, transparency and financial discipline had led to rampant corruption and the abuse of state resources (11 May). While this was a legacy the new president could hardly be blamed for, his newly proclaimed crusade produced few results. Two regional governors accused of failing to discharge their duties remained in office. The president scored, however, in terms of his own relatively modest appearance and by eliminating some of the insignia of presidential power and displaying no autocratic behaviour. This contrasted favourably with the pompous authoritarianism of his predecessor.

In the middle of the year, the biggest *financial scandals* to date came to light, involving massive fraud and abuse of public funds. The most spectacular case resulted in the suicide of Lazarus Kandara, the main party accused, under mysterious circumstances when he was being arrested (24 August). Because of the prominence of those implicated, the case became as much a policy issue as an issue of economic mismanagement and crime. It involved as a central figure Paulus Kapia, the controversial leader of the SWAPO Youth League. He had secured a parliamentary seat by being placed near the top of the party's electoral list at the discretion of Nujoma and was appointed deputy minister under Pohamba. He managed to obtain N$ 30 m from the social security commission for financial speculation by the investment company of which he was a director. The money was never returned, while some financial benefits were allegedly shared among the company's stakeholders.

This meant the court case turned into a spectacular *political controversy* over the future of this political office bearer. On 24 August, Kapia tendered his resignation as deputy minister after five months in office. His partial withdrawal led to a protracted fight within the party as to whether he should also cease to be an MP. After the politburo threatened to expel him from the party and issued an ultimatum to him, he announced his resignation on 26 October. The party president, Nujoma, confirmed on 27 October that with effect from 1 November the MP would also relinquish his parliamentary seat. Ironically, this paved the way for the return, as a backbencher, of the new national president's sidelined opponent Hamutenya, since he was the next on the party's electoral list. Amid a crowd of jubilant supporters he returned to the National Assembly on 15 November. The ousted youth league secretary was quietly rewarded with another paid job at party headquarters.

The *discovery of mass graves* during November in the former northern combat zone of Ovamboland reopened the darkest chapter of the final stages of Namibia's decolonisation when several hundred members of the armed wing of the liberation movement were killed execution-style by the South African army after moving back to Namibia. In the absence of the head of state (who was on a state visit to Germany), SWAPO's president Nujoma on several occasions dismissed any discussion of those events. At a press conference on 24 November he offered his version, namely of an imperialist conspiracy initiated by the Thatcher government to halt the further transition to Namibia's independence. During a public rally on 27 November, he blamed the editors of two newspapers for their critical reviews of the tragic incident and threatened to deal with them "as we dealt with and defeated the apartheid SA regime". The highly contentious nature of the issue was illustrated when a pro-Nujoma faction in the leadership of the SWAPO-affiliated

National Union of Namibian Workers (NUNW) issued a statement in support of Nujoma's 'patriotic history' version and lashed out at "hungry media and imperialists" (9 December). The acting secretary-general of the trade union umbrella body, who had been among the SWAPO combatants to survive the massacre, declared this statement to be unauthorised. Those in the union who had issued the statement initiated an unofficial internal meeting, which in his absence decided and subsequently publicly announced his dismissal (15 December).

The *political witch-hunt* against those who seemed to disagree with the dominant party views, in particular those of the Nujoma faction, found another prominent victim in the former trade and industry minister, Jesaya Nyamu. A long-standing activist within the exile group, he openly supported Hamutenya. He was expelled from SWAPO over notes stolen earlier from a locked drawer in his ministerial office. These contained ideas about the creation of a new party. At a press conference (13 December), a defiant Nyamu accused Nujoma of totalitarian rule, which he said had caused division and destroyed collective leadership. He publicly burned his expulsion letter. Meanwhile, a bill adopted in the National Assembly (29 November) by the majority of SWAPO parliamentarians had just conferred upon the retired head of state the official title "Founding Father of the Namibian Nation".

While several aggressive statements by SWAPO politicians indicated at best a mixed approach to *media freedom*, the country ranked 25th on the Press Freedom Index released in early November by the Paris-based watchdog organisation, Reporters Without Borders. Among the 167 countries classified, Namibia was, along with Benin, the best placed African country, followed by South Africa (ranked 31st) and far ahead of the US (44th). In contrast, the SWAPO Youth League called on 1 December for the enactment of laws by government to rein in journalists, since the misuse of the freedom of the press had allegedly reached intolerable and unacceptable levels.

Recognised freedom of expression collided on several occasions with the need to limit *hate speech*. During a public political rally on 27 August, the deputy minister of home affairs and immigration claimed that gays and lesbians had betrayed the freedom struggle, caused the HIV/AIDS pandemic and were "a slap in the face of African culture". Shortly afterwards, a local bilingual weekly newspaper published a blatantly anti-Semitic advertisement (23 September), which celebrated the death of Simon Wiesenthal as a joyful event. During a demonstration by a group of Herero led by their paramount chief in Windhoek (24 August), which demanded reparations from Germany for the genocide committed a hundred years earlier, a placard was displayed with the slogan "Kill all whites". Court action was subsequently initiated by the state against two accused persons.

With the Caprivi treason trial still pending more than six years after the accused were arrested and several reported abuses by security forces (including alleged mistreatment, torture and killings during arrests and detentions), Namibia's *human rights record* received a mixed judgement in a report released by the US government in March. While conceding general respect for human rights, it identified serious problems in several areas. The annual survey on political rights and civil liberties undertaken by Freedom House and released at the end of the year placed Namibia at two for political and three for civil rights (unchanged since 2003), on par with Lesotho (but behind South Africa and Botswana). The unabated widespread violence against women and children, as well as the misery of the San population living in abject poverty, did not add positively to the country's general image either. Amnesty International pointed in its annual overview to the horrendous degree of gendered violence, and a delegation of the African Commission on Human and People's Rights visited in July to investigate the living conditions of the San.

Foreign Affairs

Continuity was maintained by the unexpected *reappointment of the foreign minister*, Marco Hausiku, who held on to the portfolio as a result of the dismissal of Hidipo Hamutenya and who declared that he had no ambitions beyond being a temporary stand-in.

The *African dimension* continued to dominate Namibia's foreign policy orientation. President Nujoma combined participation at the AU summit in Abuja (30–31 January) with a subsequent state visit to Nigeria to discuss trade issues, among other matters. He travelled on to Angola (3–5 February), where he witnessed the formal delimitation of the maritime border between the two countries. On the occasion of Namibia's independence day, which also marked Nujoma's exit from the office as head of state, several African presidents (including most leaders from the SADC countries) attended the swearing in of the new head of state and the farewell reception for Nujoma. Among the guest speakers who honoured their retiring peer were Presidents Mugabe, Museveni and Mkapa.

Links with *SADC countries* remained high on the agenda. President Pohamba made his first state visit to neighbouring Botswana during the second half of May. Friendly relations and close collaboration with Zimbabwe, which he visited from 22 to 24 August, continued irrespective of the policy in the latter country. Both Pohamba and Nujoma (the latter as a special guest) attended the SADC summit in Gaborone (17–18 August), during which Pohamba was elected chairperson of the organ on politics, defence and security cooperation. The SADC tribunal appointed by the summit was officially inaugurated in Windhoek on 18 November and, alongside the parliamentary forum and the customs authority, became the third organ located in Namibia. In the aftermath to an official visit by Pohamba, Angola and Namibia signed a bilateral agreement (8 October) to scrap visa requirements for short-term visits between the two countries.

A visit to Tanzania (27–28 May) was used by both heads of state to issue statements in support of strengthening the continent's position as part of broader *UN reform.* Pohamba also demanded the democratisation of the UN when he addressed local diplomats (5 August) upon his return from the AU heads of government meeting in Addis Ababa. He opposed the idea of any veto right. In his speech to the 60th session of the General Assembly in New York (17 September), he reiterated the demands for adequate African representation and the abolition of any privileges for certain member states.

As one of five African presidents, Pohamba paid a *visit to the White House* on 13 June. The invitation by George W. Bush was extended in recognition of the democratic achievements of these countries. On the agenda were talks to explore greater benefits under AGOA. Pohamba used his visit to argue for LDC status for Namibia, since the average per capita income of this lower middle-income country disguised the extreme inequalities that existed as a legacy of apartheid colonialism.

Investment promotion agreements were ratified by parliament in early July with France, Italy, Austria and Vietnam. A French navy vessel arrived 30 May in Walvis Bay to establish a cooperation programme with Namibia's navy, which is mainly supported by Brazil. *Namibian-German relations* continued to be tested after commemoration initiatives during 2004 by a range of NGOs in both countries had put the genocide committed more than 100 years earlier on the political agenda. On 24 May, the German minister for economic cooperation and development announced the decision to spend an additional € 20 m over ten years as part of a reconciliation initiative offering targeted support to the Herero, Nama and Damara under the joint aegis of both governments. During August, the Namibian prime minister and the minister of information, who acted as government spokeswoman, indicated that no official communication had so far taken place on the matter. The agreement on the initiative was to be signed during the Namibian president's official state visit to Germany (28 November to 2 December). The ceremony was spoilt at the last minute by the Namibian delegation, which announced that it still needed to consult with the affected groups. Bilateral negotiations in Windhoek on continued development assistance (for which Germany, the biggest single donor country, had announced another considerable increase) were postponed from early December to the next year.

Less complicated were *ties with China*. During the parliamentary debate over the annual state budget, the minister of works announced on 21 June that the Chinese government had offered a generous grant to cover expenses for the new presidential residence under construction at the state house complex. From 16 to 18 November, a 47-member Chinese delegation of government officials and business people visited Namibia. The head of delegation welcomed Namibia's support for the Chinese position on Taiwan and human rights. He described bilateral relations as a "natural alliance". A N\$ 189 m loan for the purchase of trains and an agreement on investment promotion and protection were signed. President Pohamba accepted the invitation for a state visit, which he undertook from 16 to 21 December. He declared that its purpose was to strengthen economic ties with an old friend, which had helped Namibia to attain independence through its material, diplomatic and political support to SWAPO during the liberation struggle. In this spirit, the cabinet established an economic commission on 6 December in support of closer Chinese-Namibian cooperation.

Socioeconomic Developments

A decrease in foreign direct investment since 2003 made Namibia a net exporter of capital during the second quarter for the first time in nearly two years. According to figures released by the Bank of Namibia in its quarterly bulletin on 30 September, GDP growth for the same quarter declined to 1.1%, in contrast to 4.1% recorded during the first quarter. The *sluggish growth* was also reflected in Namibia's drop by 11 places from 52nd to 63rd in the Global Competitiveness

Report released in October by the World Economic Forum. This decline meant the country was one of the worst performers during the year.

Investor confidence was hardly buoyed by the first officially executed farm expropriation, which became effective on 1 December under the *land policy*. In March, it was reported that government had asked 14 commercial farmers with 24 farms to submit reasons why their land should not be taken. The land minister announced on 4 August that government had identified up to 18 farms for expropriation and was prepared for a "court war". Four German and one South African absentee landowner (owning a total of seven farms between them) were reported in early December to be contesting the principle of expropriation in court, banking on the investment protection treaty between their countries and Namibia.

With the closure of several companies and thousands of job losses, the year started off on a bad note for the *fishing industry*. Its seemingly bleak future was confirmed by its subsequent lacklustre performance, more insolvencies and further retrenchments. The strong local currency, in combination with the increased fuel prices, a decline in fish biomass and the allocated fishing quota, which reduced total allowable catches, had a disastrous effect.

Rumours continued that as an effect of the ending of the WTO agreement on textiles and clothing, the foreign investments made under AGOA by a Malaysian enterprise in *textile and apparel production* established locally as Ramatex would be terminated. Government downplayed labour disputes at the textile factories and the investor denied any intentions of withdrawing. Both blamed the trade union for spoiling the image of the enterprise and thereby risking the marketing of its products. Ultimately, the closure of the subsidiary Rhino garment factory, which employed more than 1,600 local workers, was confirmed on 4 April.

Four petroleum exploration licences awarded to three companies on 23 August sparked off much unfounded hype about an oil boom, fuelled further by another two licences issued during the remainder of the year. Plans to develop the Kudu gas project off the coast, instead of further pursuing the stalled Epupa hydro project, also made progress. Positive trends were registered in parts of the *mining sector* due to increased demand for uranium ore. More than 800 workers at the British Rio Tinto-owned Rössing uranium mine, whose lifeline had been under threat for three years, were relieved to learn in December that the production period had been extended until 2016. The planned annual production of 3,800 tonnes had been met and the targeted volume was increased to 4,000 tonnes for the next two years. Plans for opening a uranium mine at Langer Heinrich by the Australian company, Paladin Resources, proceeded despite massive objections by environmental groups: the ground-breaking ceremony took place on 15 September. The minister of mines and energy reiterated in parliament on 21 October that the country should further develop its eight known uranium deposits into mines.

The *national budget* tabled by the reappointed finance minister in parliament on 12 May was widely viewed as a sign of fiscal continuity under the new president, but met with little enthusiasm from local economists. The budget deficit expected for 2004–05 would add to the debt of N$ 12 bn by the end of the fiscal year (31 March). Spending for 2005–06 was projected to amount N$ 12.8 bn, income to N$ 12.3 bn, with a deficit of N$ 448.5 m or 1.2% of GDP. Statutory payments for accumulated debts were estimated to be above N$ 1.1 bn, slightly below 10% of the budget. While the minister talked of the need to restructure spending, the local Institute for Public Policy Research (IPPR) reported "precious little evidence of this happening". Namibia had not been able to make efficient use of a number of positive economic assets since independence, as the same institute noted at a conference on 5 December. Unemployment had almost doubled during the 15 years since then to above 30%, while public spending on a bloated civil service had increased. Most of the budget was spent on salaries rather than development, while accumulated debt amounted to one-third of GDP.

Additional pressure on the public purse came from the socioeconomic *effects of HIV/AIDS*. By mid-year, the health ministry managed to provide some 17,000 of an estimated 56,000 patients with the needed anti-retroviral treatment. It was estimated that 21% of the population age group of 15 to 49 years was HIV positive. According to a UN report, only Botswana and Uganda had a similarly high rate. Soaring health expenditure was but one effect of this situation. As a study by the Namibian Economic Policy Research Unit (NEPRU) presented in October revealed, the pandemic also to a large extent affected the survival strategies of subsistence farmers in communal areas, who were no longer able to produce the food they needed. Nearly half of the 144 households surveyed in the Oshana, Oshikoto and Okavango regions depended upon the pensions of N$ 300 for which those above the age of 65 were eligible, while one-fifth of the households relied on drought relief from the state.

A coalition of churches and NGOs was inspired by a South African initiative to lobby for a Basic Income Grant (BIC) of N$ 100 monthly for every Namibian as a measure to ease *poverty*, but received no support from the government. Indeed, the minister for gender equality and child welfare responded on 5 October to an opposition motion in parliament to increase the monthly state pensions to N$ 500 by maintaining that pensioners received "endless benefits". Data collected by the national planning commission estimated that 70% of the population lived below the poverty line. According to a WFP report issued on 1 July, a total of 60,000 people were estimated to suffer from hunger. The UN Human Development Report released in September noted that Namibia still has a Gini co-efficient of 0.71, making it the country with the world's most marked income inequality. A week earlier, the UN country assessment warned that a humanitarian crisis was unfolding largely because of the triple threat of HIV/AIDS, food insecurity and the ineffective delivery of critical social services.

Namibia in 2006

This year, there were no spectacular political events to report. President Pohamba pursued a low-profile policy aimed at reconciling the different factions in the SWAPO party, which continued to dominate the political scene unchallenged. Since Pohamba took office in March 2005, there have been no cabinet reshuffles. However, the internal power struggles continued unabated and showed that the different factions remained in fierce competition for control of political power. In foreign policy, closer links to China emerged as the most remarkable feature. Concerning socioeconomic performance, little improved for the majority of people despite the first projected annual budget surplus since independence, while the self-enrichment schemes for the new elite flourished.

Domestic Politics

The main theme in domestic affairs remained the question of which of the *two presidents* really exercised power and governed the country: the former head of state Sam Nujoma, who remained president of the dominant (though much divided) SWAPO party or his own candidate for succession, the elected head of state Hifikepunye Pohamba. In public, the new head of state maintained a loyal attitude towards Nujoma as the party president and tolerated his predecessor's interference in substantive matters. The two did not engage in public power struggles, but it was evident that Pohamba sought to heal the wounds inflicted in the bitter inner party power struggles over Nujoma's successor as head of state. Pohamba reappointed some of the ousted party members into higher positions and did not pursue a confrontational policy. The inner-party conflicts, however, simmered on. All eyes were on Nujoma, who prepared to secure his party presidency for at least another term at the next party congress (end of 2007). His cohorts started visible mobilisation while other factions did likewise in an effort to prevent this eventuality, all at the expense of a secure and stable policy environment. Speculation and strategic moves dominated the scene, while President Pohamba at least publicly stayed out the fray and tried to limit the damage. In a symbolic encounter, which received much media coverage, the motorcades of the two presidents travelling in opposite directions met unexpectedly on the tar road in northern Namibia on 5 December. Reportedly, the motorcade of Namibia's head of state had to make way for that of his party president.

The *internal power struggles* were reproduced on a number of fronts. The politics of firm control by the dominant party faction acting on behalf of Nujoma resulted in continued interference in local government matters, where elected office bearers on district or town levels and party members elected to regional or local party offices were replaced if they did not have the confidence of the Nujoma faction. The SWAPO-affiliated National Union of Namibian Workers (NUNW) dismissed its secretary-general for the critical stance he had taken earlier towards Nujoma. The 4th national NUNW congress, which preceded May Day, was marred by dissent and tumult, and delegates from the teachers' and the mineworkers' unions walked out in protest over the procedures adopted, which prevented dissenting views from being voiced. Leading independent-minded trade unionists were replaced by Nujoma loyalists. The leadership of member unions – notably the Namibian national teachers' union – was subsequently also replaced by Nujoma followers. At the congress of the SWAPO women's council on 8–10 December, a similar revamp occurred when one of Nujoma's confidantes, the deputy minister of health, was appointed new secretary of the influential body. She replaced a long-time activist alleged to be an 'imperialist' who had insulted the 'old man' (Nujoma). All these manipulative interventions pointed at the forthcoming SWAPO congress in 2007, which decides the next party president and indirectly also the presidential candidate for the elections in late 2009.

Nujoma remained publicly active at the party level. On 1 July, he blamed the white community for committing a crime against humanity and warned the British they would face consequences for interfering in Zimbabwe: "You touch Zimbabwe, you touch SWAPO", he said. Speaking on 15 July, he threatened that Namibia could use its uranium resources to "make its own atomic bombs" if external forces "create[d] nonsense". Upset by the demands of a group of former SWAPO combatants (see below), he allegedly made veiled death threats to members of this committee at a party meeting on 30 July. This prompted the UN special rapporteur on human rights to inquire of the foreign ministry in a letter of 10 August as to the substance of these allegations. On 3 August, Nujoma provoked students of the University of Namibia and the polytechnic to walk out in protest – a hitherto unknown form of open defiance, which illustrated the growing frustration over the offensive behaviour displayed by the 'founding father of the nation'. Nevertheless, at the annual SWAPO central committee meeting on 16–17 December, Nujoma declared that leaders must ensure that they promoted party and national unity, patriotism and solidarity and must embrace democratic norms and principles in their intentions, deeds and actions. He also dismissed claims by "some treacherous elements" and some local media that the party was divided.

Anti-corruption initiatives were a priority in President Pohamba's policies. On 27 March, he launched a zero-tolerance campaign, which laid the basis for cooperation between the newly established anti-corruption commission, the office of the ombudsman and various civil society organisations. However, self-enrichment schemes in the private sector and in the public services reached unprecedented heights. Black Economic Empowerment (BEE) and affirmative action schemes served as smokescreens for dubious, if not fraudulent practices. Financial scandals were under investigation in a number of parastatals and state institutions such as the Offshore Development Cooperation, which reported that Namibian dollars (N$) 100 m had gone missing. Misappropriation of funds in the social security commission resulted in over 50 employees being arrested during the year. Forensic investigation into the government institutions pension fund's development capital portfolio took place following the discovery that more than N$ 600 m were earlier allocated to BEE business operations, with many of these not repaying the preferential loans.

While the ousted CEO of the agricultural bank declared in mid-October in a labour lawsuit that his monthly salary of N$ 83,000 was "mid-range" and "moderate", hundreds of disappointed *war veterans* had been publicly mobilised since mid-year in pursuit of adequate compensation. President Pohamba dismissed their material claims as excessive in a televised address to the nation on 4 August and argued that meeting their demands would amount to an estimated annual expenditure of N$ 6 bn or 40% of the budget. However, government showed its concern by appointing the SWAPO party's secretary-general to a newly created portfolio for war veterans. In contrast, the party's president, Nujoma, categorically dismissed claims by the war veterans that in the course of negotiating independence they had been promised material compensation for their sacrifices during the struggle.

Foreign Affairs

Namibia remained committed to friendly relations with *other African countries* but sceptical about the APRM. The foreign minister reiterated on 10 March that while NEPAD would be considered part of the continental policy Namibia rejected the APRM. At the end of April, Botswana's President Mogae opened the town council's civic centre in the northern Namibian main town Oshakati and pointed out that both governments shared a commitment to decentralisation as a form of regional development. Tanzania's President Kikwete used his visit in mid-April to hold talks between the two governments as chair and deputy chair respectively of the SADC organ on politics, defence and security and to call for strong support for the forthcoming elections in DR Congo. On 26 April, President Pohamba opened a SADC consultative conference in Windhoek with all member states in attendance to discuss sub-regional development as well as politics, defence and security. He visited the Republic of Congo for three days at the end of October and signed four agreements with his counterpart Sassou Nguesso. The Namibia-Angola joint commission on defence and security held its 13th session in early July in northern Namibia. On 21 September, the minister of information held a press conference in the presence of diplomats from Angola, South Africa and Botswana to clarify that a document circulating and claiming that there was an Angolan-Namibian 'defence protocol' was a fabrication. The document suggested that there was a military pact on bilateral assistance in the event of military conflict with other SADC states. Another row erupted over a visit by the deputy minister of lands to Zimbabwe in June. According to local media reports, he had expressed admiration for Zimbabwe's land policy. The government issued a press release at the end of June that this did not imply a shift in land policies in Namibia and that the minister was quoted out of context.

In May, relations with *South Africa* improved with the drafting of an agreement on the contested issue of water use from the Orange River, the common border. On 21 November, the 6th presidential meeting on economics between Namibia and South Africa took place in Windhoek. Presidents Pohamba and Mbeki updated the bilateral economic agreement, which included a total of 48 transborder projects. The further exploration and utilisation of the offshore Kudu gas field along the southern coastline of Namibia was identified as a priority to contribute to the sub-regional energy supply. The talks also included discussions on special arrangements to allow Mozambique, Malawi and Zambia limited benefits from SACU.

Namibia's role in the *UN* featured prominently. On 27 January, President Pohamba demanded a bigger role for Africa on the

Security Council by supporting the call for five non-permanent seats. He emphasised that Namibia's contribution to peace missions in Liberia, Sudan and Sierra Leone demonstrated the country's multilateralism at all levels. A fifth peacekeeping contingent of 610 soldiers left for Liberia at the end of September. Addressing the UN General Assembly on 20 September, Pohamba urged all parties in the Sudan to respect the transition from the AU to the UN peacekeeping force. But Namibia's role in the UN was not free of controversy. At the end of March, a government decision to object to the participation of local NGOs in the General Assembly's special session on AIDS caused uproar among advocacy groups. Namibia's ambassador to the UN provoked adverse international headlines when he proposed on 28 November on behalf of several African countries the deferment of adoption of the declaration on the rights of *indigenous peoples* until the end of the General Assembly session to allow for further consultations. Observers considered this a strategic move to prevent the adoption of the original declaration. Namibia was backed by Botswana, several other African countries, Canada, Australia, New Zealand and Russia. However, the 14 African member countries of the UN Human Rights Council that had approved the declaration on 29 June were among those recommending adoption. Finland, on behalf of the EU, urged a vote against delaying the declaration. Several human rights groups and similar agencies advocating indigenous minority rights harshly criticised Namibia, which like Botswana is accused of neglecting the local Bushmen (San) communities.

Friendly relations with *China* were consolidated. The ministry of foreign affairs issued a statement in early March confirming the government's support for the one-China policy. More than 20 business people were included, along with the president and his entourage, in the Namibian delegation that toured Singapore from 30 October and then attended the Sino-African summit in Beijing. The trip was described as an 'eye opener' and Chinese industry was viewed as eager to do business with its Namibian counterparts, notably in the mining sector. A total of seven twinning arrangements between Chinese and Namibian towns underscored the exceptionally close ties. *Russian interests* were evident in the inaugural session on 27–28 July in Windhoek of the Namibia-Russian intergovernmental commission on trade and economic cooperation. *Cuban* assistance continued in the health sector, in which 170 Cuban health professionals worked during the year. Military cooperation with the US took place in September, when Namibian defence force officers received training as international peacekeepers. Namibia was among the 21 countries that were in mid-October again declared eligible for US military training programmes. Their participation was earlier denied because of their refusal to sign an agreement with the US administration that would exempt Americans from prosecution by the International Criminal Court.

The special relations with *Germany* were underscored in Windhoek in mid-May in the bilateral talks on development cooperation: these resulted in a further increase in development aid by the single largest donor country. On 26 October, Namibia's parliament adopted without any objections a motion recalling the genocide under German colonial rule a century ago and demanding dialogue with Germany on reparations. In December, the implementation of a special reconciliation initiative by the German government was advertised. Not considered to be reparations, the tender invited consultancy services to define the framework for a € 20 m development programme over a ten year period. This initiative had earlier been blocked by the Namibian government, which had wanted further clarification. As the tender specified, "the special initiative is meant for development projects in areas and for communities that had 'historic ties' with the German colonial government and which the present German government considers as a special moral and political responsibility towards Namibia to aid the said communities." The Namibian government reportedly requested that the San communities be included as beneficiaries of this initiative.

Socioeconomic Developments

Minister of Finance Saara Kuugongelwa-Amadhila tabled the *annual budget* for 2006–07 on 16 March. It was the first since independence that presented a balanced account and predicted a surplus for the year and was described by her as "pro-poor, pro-growth". The only feature that possibly deserved such praise was the announced increase in the monthly pension for the elderly from N$ 300 to N$ 370. It became effective half a year later and was the first increase since 2004. Total expenditure for the financial year (April to March) was expected to increase by 18.6% to N$ 15.2 bn, with income expected to increase by 23.6% to N$ 15.25 bn through favourable revenue flows from, in particular, the SACU pool: these were expected to increase by 65% to some N$ 6.1 bn. However, dependence on these revenues at the same time showed the continued vulnerability of the Namibian state budget, especially as SACU revenue is likely to decline considerably with new free trade arrangements. Against the background of this *unsustainable revenue base*, the continued expansion of the budget was called into question, while local economists criticised the budget for bringing about neither long-term poverty reduction nor incentives to stimulate local economic growth and investment. The *additional budget* announced on 8 November adjusted the expected total government spending for the financial year to N$ 15.28 bn, with a much higher budget surplus of N$ 799 m.

In contrast to this positive balance, the *debt burden* remained a challenge. Government's debt-to-revenue ratio had soared from 7% in 1992 to more than 100%. Repayment of interest on debt equalled around 10% of budget allocations to the ministries of defence and of health and social services, which both received about the same allocations. For the purchase of farms under the land reform and resettlement policy, N$ 50 m was allocated. In contrast, slightly more was earmarked for security services, while double the amount was put aside to finance the soaring costs of the new state house complex (built by Chinese and North Korean contractors) and slightly more for the protection of VIPs. In its analysis, the Institute for Public Policy Research (IPPR) characterised the budget as "piecemeal and opportunistic reform rather than change according to a well thought-out, long-term plan." Expenditure was expected to rise to 35.6% of GDP. While the finance minister described the civil service as bloated and as unsustainable on the basis of current expenditure (with capital expenditure always on the low side), the public service wage bill for the year was estimated to rise again from N\$ 5.5 bn to N\$ 6.1 bn. The finance minister repeated her warnings in earlier budget speeches that a continued increase of the country's debt load placed a heavy burden on future generations – but increased expenditure and borrowing. As the IPPR concluded, the government continued to spend every cent it could lay its hands on. The state-owned Namibia Post and Telecom Holdings (NPTH) obtained additional income on 25 July when it finalised the country's biggest commercial deal of the year with the sale of 34% of the share capital in Mobile Telecommunications (MTC) to Portugal Telecom for N\$ 1.02 bn.

Article IV discussions were held by an *IMF mission* from 6–14 November in Windhoek. The statement issued on 14 November commended authorities for the fiscal consolidation over the last two years that had reduced the fiscal deficit from over 7% of GDP to close to balance. It critically noted that one-off receipts from the partial privatisation of the state-owned MTC could have been used to reduce public debt and recommended continued reduction of the public debt ratio. This was required because of the projected substantial decline in SACU revenue and the country's significant public investment needs in health, education, poverty reduction and infrastructure. The statement warned that "more determined efforts [were] needed to reduce poverty so as to maintain social cohesion."

The outgoing local *EU representative* voiced his *criticism* of the government's poor planning, misjudgements and haphazard decision-making and noted that these harmed investor confidence. In an interview published by the state-owned 'New Era' (30 June), he stated his impression that the government executed "development plans without proper planning and the necessary research needed for the implementation of its socio-economic projects." He further maintained that implementation of aid projects was hampered by red tape and that investors had complained of the risks of doing business in Namibia.

Such criticism, combined with the increase in graft scandals and corruption, was also reflected in Namibia's *international ranking*. The World Economic Forum released its global competitiveness report at the end of November and the local business community noted with concern that Namibia's ranking had dropped from 79 to 84. According to TI's corruption perceptions index presented on 6 November, Namibia dropped from 47th to 55th. In the UNDP HDI, released in mid-November, Namibia remained in 125th position.

The *energy supply* remained high on the agenda, as Namibia imported about half its electricity, mainly from South Africa. One of the biggest single investments in infrastructure development in the annual budget was the N$ 250 m allocated for the development of the offshore Kudu gas power project to avert the imminent power crisis, which was evident in the increasingly irregular power supply from South Africa. Delivery failures caused black-outs in parts of Namibia and forced local electricity distributors to implement contingency plans. On 14 December, the CEO of Namibia's parastatal energy provider Nampower announced in Windhoek, at the opening of a working meeting with energy utilities from Botswana, Mozambique, South Africa, Zimbabwe and Zambia, that the *Kudu gas field* would be developed further in collaboration with South Africa's Eskom and the South Africa-based continental energy company Tullow Oil. He added that a Caprivi link would connect Namibia at an estimated cost of N$ 3 bn with Zambia, Botswana and Zimbabwe. Furthermore, Namibia and Angola planned to undertake a study for a hydroelectric power project on the Kunene river (their joint border) and Nampower explored a western corridor project providing a link to the Inga project on the Congo River in the DR Congo. The permanent secretary of the ministry of mines and energy disclosed to a local newspaper at year's end that government had decided to use its own uranium resources to produce nuclear power. Already on 30 January he had unsettled participants at a renewable energy workshop exploring the possibilities of solar and wind power when he announced that nuclear energy would be an option.

While the ailing fisheries sector was unable to recover from the setbacks in 2005 and the quota for the total allowable catch remained low, the *mining sector* thrived. Diamond production remained the most important single source of income to the economy, but there was notable diversification as a result of the favourable world market for the country's other minerals and metals. Scorpion Zinc and Rössing Uranium alone contributed 36% of the mining sector's total income (and 49% of non-diamond mining income), which peaked at N\$ 11.4 bn for the year, an increase of 52% as against 2005. The lower exchange rate of the N\$ against the US\$ as well as increased demand by Asian economies contributed to the favourable conditions. Namibia produced some 7.5% of the world's *uranium* output, with a new mine at Langer Heinrich soon to be operational. At that point, Namibia was expected to account for 10% of the world's uranium, a figure that was likely to increase further to 15% given all the concessions issued, much to the disquiet of environmental groups, which vainly tried to limit the damage. *Zinc* was produced in the Anglo American-owned Scorpion mine and the Exxaro subsidiary Rosh Pinah mine, with huge profit margins due to world market price increases of more than 100% over 2005.

Notwithstanding such favourable conditions, the marginalisation of large parts of Namibia's population continued unabated. In early December, the local UNICEF office presented a study that showed a continued marked increase in *violence* against women, children and elderly people. Even young children and seniors were not spared rape, physical abuse and other forms of violence.

The report suggested that women and girls were under constant siege wherever they went, and held attitudes of male superiority responsible. The imbalance in gender relations was a local focus of the acting secretary-general of the Namibian Red Cross when the organisation presented its global report on catastrophes on 14 December. Another area of concern was the situation of an estimated 120,000 orphans, most of whom had lost their parents to AIDS.

Another worrying feature was the continued destitution of the *San population.* The roughly 32,000 members of the various San communities had by far the lowest average income and 60% were dependent on food aid. Most of these communities formed part of the local populations in the Omaheke and Caprivi regions, on which the national planning commission presented regional poverty profiles in mid-year. According to these reports, a quarter of the Omaheke population lived in extreme poverty, while 40% of the Caprivi region's households were considered poor (with the national average 29.1%). The desperate situation of some San communities was brought into the limelight by the local newspaper, 'The Namibian' (14 March). It disclosed that San communities in western Caprivi had out of sheer hunger eaten mouldy rice distributed to them as food aid, even though officials told them it was unfit for human consumption. Samples tested afterwards in the state veterinary laboratory proved the rice to be unfit for both human and animal consumption.

In marked contrast to bread and butter issues, there was exceptional hype over *Hollywood celebrities* when Angelina Jolie stayed with Brad Pitt for several weeks in a coastal resort to give birth to their daughter on 28 May. They received VIP treatment, including the screening of all journalists trying to enter the country during the period and police action against any person suspected of trying to intrude on the couple's privacy. According to the deputy minister for tourism, the government offered the newborn child Namibian citizenship. The frenzy culminated in proposals to declare the birthday a public holiday. Less spectacular were visits later in the year by the British Prince Harry and Sir Richard Branson.

Meanwhile, the initiative by a church-based coalition demanding a *Basic Income Grant* (BIG) received less favourable response. The BIG coalition asked for an unconditional grant of N$ 100 to every Namibian under retirement age. This would amount to 2% of GDP, but was rejected by the cabinet in May.

Namibia in 2007

The year culminated with the biggest change to the national political landscape since independence, with the collapse of the official
opposition party as a result of internal differences, while several
high-ranking members of the former liberation movement and
dominant ruling party, the South West Africa People's Organisation
(SWAPO), registered their own new political party. The SWAPO
congress elected the head of state as its new party president. Sam
Nujoma, SWAPO president since the founding of the movement and
head of state for 15 years, did not stand for election again. By year's
end, Namibia's political map was both the same as before and very
different.

The country's foreign policy persisted with its Look East orientation and the expansion of economic relations with new partners
interested in accessing the natural wealth. In socioeconomic terms,
the resource-rich country benefited from the soaring world market
prices for several of its main export items, mainly in the mining sector. The annual state budget for the first time made provision for
a surplus for a second consecutive year, but the mid-term perspectives remained precarious in the absence of any meaningful signs of
redistribution of wealth.

Domestic Politics

In the absence of any elections, domestic politics were characterised by spectacular turmoil on the party political landscape. During
its party congress on 4 and 5 May, the Congress of Democrats
(CoD) became deeply divided over controversial elections for its
leadership positions, elections that resulted in a *split in the official
opposition* (a formal status based on the Westminster model and
attached to the biggest opposition party in parliament). Both of the

© KONINKLIJKE BRILL NV, LEIDEN, 2016 | DOI 10.1163/9789004321571_006

two leading founding members of this party, which emerged during 1999 mainly from the ranks of the former liberation movement SWAPO, had earlier been deputy ministers in the SWAPO government. At this year's congress, they were openly at loggerheads over the party's presidency, with accusations of tribalism and mismanagement being exchanged. Party President Ben Ulenga claimed re-election after winning the votes of 155 out of 309 delegates in a second-round vote against his opponent Ignatius Shixwameni, the party's secretary general. About 100 delegates supporting the latter, including three of the party's five MPs, walked out in protest. They accused the Ulenga faction of manipulating the composition of the delegates. The remaining congress participants continued with the elections and filled all the posts in the party's top structure with Ulenga loyalists. Further disputes over party property, the portion of party finances allocated by the state and the party's other assets bedevilled any efforts at reconciliation and the rivalry escalated further into irreversible rifts. The recommendations of an independent audit panel, which sought compromise solutions to overcome the crisis, were not implemented. Instead, after Ulenga announced that the dissidents had been expelled, the opponents went to court. While the matter dragged on for the remainder of the year, the opponents remained in their positions due to an interim court order. Both factions claimed to represent the legitimate CoD. In a surprise move, Shixwameni announced his resignation from the party with immediate effect on 10 December, sparking rumours that he intended to establish his own party.

Meanwhile, while the CoD unravelled, a *new opposition party* made headlines. It was the long expected result of fundamental divisions within SWAPO. These had become visible with the side-lining of the party faction that had in mid-2004 supported Hidipo Hamutenya, the former foreign minister, as possible successor to Namibia's first head of state and SWAPO President Sam Nujoma. The rift culminated with the expulsion of former Trade Minister Jesaya Nyamu from the party at the end of 2006. Both Hamutenya and Nyamu were of the first generation of exile politicians and were members of the party's inner circle. On 2 November, the Rally for Democracy and Progress (RDP) was officially registered as a new party with the Electoral Commission of Namibia (ECN) after Nyamu applied for registration in August. After months of unconfirmed speculation and rumours of a split in SWAPO, constantly denied by party officials, the news came as a bombshell. Several higher ranking SWAPO members declared their intention to join the new party. At a press conference on 8 November, Hidipo Hamutenya announced his resignation from SWAPO and as a member of parliament and his intention to join the RDP, of which he became acting president, with Jesaya Nyamu becoming acting secretary general. On 17 November, the official launch of the party took place at a public rally in Katutura, the former township of the capital Windhoek. The party seemed able to make inroads into the hitherto uncontested SWAPO strongholds in parts of the former Ovamboland in northern Namibia. The region is considered decisive to any political dominance, given that more than half of the country's electorate originates there. Historically, SWAPO grew up among contract workers from Ovamboland in the 1950s and had never lost its firm control over the area. RDP officials announced that their short-term political goal would be to break SWAPO's two-thirds majority in the National Assembly in the next parliamentary elections scheduled for late 2009, but had not spelled out their political platform by year's end. However, high unemployment; the lack of educational, health and other social services; and the unsatisfactory distribution of wealth quickly emerged as campaign issues. An initial political rally held on 9 December in the deep-sea harbour town of Walvis Bay, the only other industrial urban centre outside Windhoek and home to the fishing industry and a high number of organised workers, drew a large crowd.

Prime Minister Nahas Angula was quoted on 7 November in the state-owned daily newspaper that the RDP was a "paper party" and no threat, but would jeopardise peace and stability. He expressed concern over the security of the country since the political culture in the four north-central regions (the former Ovamboland) does not allow for peaceful political activity. The governing party reacted to the RDP with an internal campaign tantamount to a *SWAPO witch-hunt*. The director of the ECN was accused of not alerting the government or party about the registration process and was subsequently branded as a traitor and clandestine RDP follower. The party's Youth League spearheaded the internal vendetta against anyone suspected of not toeing the party line and asked for the dismissal of the ECN director. In mid-November, the party's secretary general confirmed to a local newspaper that an oath had been drafted that, once adopted, would require all party members to swear absolute loyalty to SWAPO.

The announcement of the establishment of RDP coincided with the final preparations for the fourth ordinary *SWAPO congress* since independence (27–30 November). The gathering of over 400 party delegates from all regions of the country, during which the party leadership was elected, was preceded by frantic efforts to eliminate delegates with suspected RDP leanings. As a result, several elected delegates were replaced at short notice. After much speculation about whether SWAPO's founding president, Sam Nujoma, would seek re-election and remain in official charge of the party, the party's secretary general announced on 9 November that the politburo had nominated Namibia's President Hifikepunye Pohamba for election as the party's president and the former Prime Minister Hage Geingob as vice president. Geingob had left politics temporarily after a row with Sam Nujoma and taken a position with a World Bank-affiliated Africa agency in Washington before returning to Namibian politics in 2005 as a backbencher in the National Assembly. The party's central committee, which met on 25–26 November ahead of the congress, confirmed the nominations, while Nujoma, at the opening of the congress on 27 November, confirmed he was stepping down as party president and would not hold any other position in the party. This marked the *end of an era*, even though the congress resolved that Nujoma would retain unrestricted access to and unlimited participation in any of the party's meetings. None of the party's top positions was contested, and President Pohamba was adopted by a motion at the congress as the party's official candidate in the next presidential elections in late 2009. This ended further speculation about the future candidate and strengthened his leadership and authority. The return of former Prime Minister Geingob to the top echelons of the party sparked speculations as to whether he was being groomed as the successor to Pohamba as both head of state and party president. Current Prime Minister Angula, who had played a considerable strategic role in the process by which Pohamba had been nominated as successor to Nujoma, remained surprisingly inconspicuous and seemed to have no bright future. After 47 years as president of SWAPO, the 78-year old Nujoma was honoured at a rally in Katutura on 1 December, where an impressive crowd of several thousand cheering people paid him farewell.

Other election results from the congress indicated further *changes in SWAPO*. For the first time since independence, both the party's 21-member politburo and the 83-member central committee had no white representatives. In both organs, several long-serving, high-ranking activists and political heavyweights were eliminated. They were suspected of being not unsympathetic to the new RDP or of other critical tendencies regarding the party's dominant course. All those in the old guard considered to be reliable kept their positions. Newly elected into both influential organs was Utoni Nujoma, deputy minister of justice and son of the party's and country's first president. Losers in the elections were the women: while they represented almost half the congress delegates, only three were elected to the politburo (previously four), and only 18 (previously 19) to the central committee. The congress adopted 30 resolutions in total, dealing with various policy matters that were also of national interest. Among the contentious issues dealt with was the resolution that government establish a media council to regulate the activities and operation of the media in the country.

A topic that gave rise to heated controversy during the year was *national reconciliation* and coming to terms with the past. The unresolved issue of past injustices fuelled new debate when it emerged mid-year that the National Society for Human Rights (NSHR) had made a submission to the International Criminal Court (ICC) to investigate the responsibility of Sam Nujoma and a few other SWAPO officials for human rights violations committed in exile. The public outcry over this "felony" culminated in death threats to the director of the NSHR, who had himself been a victim of internal SWAPO repressions while in exile. Several SWAPO-affiliated bodies, including the trade union and the students' organisations, demanded publicly that unpatriotic elements such as the NSHR, some of the media as well as individual scholars be taken to task. During his speech on Heroes' Day (26 August), President Pohamba lashed out at what he called misguided individuals and organisations acting in concert to disrupt peace and stability. At an earlier public rally he had offered dissenting voices a one-way air ticket to leave the country. This stridency was in stark contrast to the soft and conciliatory messages Pohamba usually relays. Similar outbursts against voices critical of party and government policy were also evident in a series of parliamentary debates during which higher ranking SWAPO politicians did not shy away from lambasting "misguided elements".

Public criticism of government policy was also cited as justification for introducing stricter state controls over *media freedom* during debates in the National Council, the National Assembly and in the adoption of the resolution on the matter by the SWAPO congress. At a workshop in mid-September, the minister of information and broadcasting declared that freedom of expression and access to information should not be used to breed insecurity. In response to the ongoing debate and the SWAPO congress resolution, the Namibian Editors' Forum, the Media Institute of Southern Africa and other local institutions rejected all state interference in the constitutionally enshrined freedom of the media.

Foreign Affairs

Friendly relations with neighbouring countries remained a priority, although at times the differences within the sub-region were difficult to reconcile. This became evident in the case of *Zimbabwe*. President Mugabe visited on 27–28 February and signed a series of bilateral agreements. The visit was declared to be a symbol of the enduring friendship between the two countries, notwithstanding public protest by some local rights activists. Their protest over the massive outbreak of renewed oppression of the political opposition from 11 March onwards resulted in the protesters being banned from presenting a petition to the Zimbabwean high commission. An opposition party motion in parliament to discuss the Zimbabwean situation was dismissed by the SWAPO majority and the foreign minister declared such a debate would amount to interference in the internal affairs of another country. In contrast to this display of solidarity with the besieged regime, Zambian President Mwanawasa, who was guest of honour at the Independence Day celebrations (21 March), used the opportunity to make highly critical public statements about the Zimbabwean government's policy and compared Zimbabwe to the sinking Titanic. As the host country, Namibia did not dissociate itself from the guest's remarks. When, however, in August prominent government critic John Makumbe, a scholar from the University of Zimbabwe, was to give a public lecture at the University of Namibia (which had been announced publicly long before), the office of the vice-chancellor cancelled the lecture at short notice reportedly on the instruction of the former head of state, who is the university's chancellor. As a result, the lecture was held at a different venue and drew a large audience.

Relations with *Angola* remained close. The Kunene transboundary water supply project established between the two countries announced in July that the infrastructure for the supply of potable water would be established in southern Angola and north-central Namibia with financial support from Germany. The importance of the project was emphasised during Angolan President Dos Santos's visit for official talks with Pohamba (24 October). The governments signed 11 agreements in different sectors. A final communiqué by the presidents also called on Western countries to lift the sanctions against Zimbabwe. Earlier the same month, Pohamba had already made a similar statement during a working visit to Japan (13–18 October). President Mbeki underlined the good relations with *South Africa* with his state visit on 30–31 October. This followed a short meeting between Mbeki and Pohamba in Tshwane/Pretoria on 11 October. Of common concern was the severe power shortage facing both countries and the plan to establish a power plant along the Orange River, but the use of nuclear energy and the gas reserves off the coast was also explored. In a speech to the National Assembly, Mbeki noted that the common history of both countries under apartheid, an experience that cemented "ties that bind us to a common destiny".

Regional ties were also cultivated through a conference hosted by the minister of fisheries for his Angolan and South African counterparts in July as the first meeting of the tripartite Benguela Current Commission (BCC). The purpose of the meeting was discussion of common interests regarding the protection of the Atlantic Ocean biosphere. On 12 October, the three presidents of Namibia, Botswana and South Africa jointly opened the Mata Mata border post between South Africa and Namibia, which had been closed for 17 years, and the expanded Kgalagadi Peace Park. The park was expected to become a popular tourist destination, to the benefit of all three countries.

The special ties with *China* were highlighted in late September at a farewell function for the departing Chinese ambassador. The two countries had signed some 20 agreements over the past four years and trade volume had tripled to $ 250 m between 2003 and 2006. Chinese grants led to the construction of several public buildings by Chinese companies. President Hu Jintao had visited Namibia on 5 February as part of his tour to several African countries. Namibia expressed its support for the One-China policy and opposed the establishment of a Taiwan-Africa forum. Wider ties with *Russia* were initiated during a visit by Prime Minister Fradkov in March, when his delegation sought closer collaboration in energy matters (see below). Another Russian delegation of almost 30 members, led by the country's minister of natural resources, attended the two-day inaugural session of the Namibia-Russia intergovernmental commission on trade and economic cooperation (27 and 28 July) in Windhoek.

Relations with *Western countries* produced little noteworthy news. Following a cabinet decision on 11 October, two US citizens were deported from Namibia on 12 October after being declared illegal immigrants. They were allegedly trying to recruit Namibians with military training for assignments in Iraq and Afghanistan on behalf of the Special Operations Consulting-Security Management Group company. The local branch of this enterprise was also closed. In a public statement on 30 November, the Swedish chargé d'affaires in Namibia dismissed allegations that her country had financially supported the establishment of the new RDP opposition party. As a result of bilateral German-Namibian negotiations in Bonn and Berlin (5–8 November), it was finally agreed that the special German Namibia Initiative, whose implementation was pending, would receive an additional € 20 m over three to five years. The country originally refused to sign the EPA negotiated along with the SADC minor configuration. However, under pressure from local lobby groups afraid of losing preferential market access to the EU (for beef, for instance) the government reversed its policy at short notice and entered an interim EPA with Brussels in December. Earlier, in the middle of the year, the EPA controversy had resulted in the sacking of an economist with the Namibian agency Meatco for his publicly expressed criticism of the EPAs.

At the *UN* General Assembly on 3 October, Foreign Minister Marco Hausiku delivered a speech in which he appealed for more development aid. He declared that Namibia's ranking as a lower middle-income country was misleading, since the distribution of income and assets is among the most unequal in the world. He also warned of the serious consequences Namibia faces as a result of climate change.

Socioeconomic Developments

In terms of the macroeconomic performance and corresponding indicators, this was a *sound fiscal year*. This fact was duly applauded in the IMF executive board's concluding statement on the article IV consultations for 2007. Most strikingly, the fiscal balance for the year 2006–07 (ending 31 March) had moved into surplus as a result of high SACU receipts and tighter management of expenditures. It was estimated that the fiscal surplus was 2.6% of GDP with the public debt reduced considerably, thereby meeting the government's target ceiling of less than 25% of GDP. The current account balance was estimated to have risen to 18.5% of GDP (comparing favourably with the 15.9% in 2006 and especially with the 5.5% in 2005) and international reserves (in terms of months of imports) were estimated to have grown from 2.1 to 2.8. High unemployment and poverty rates were a reason for concern, as were the continued vulnerability to economic shocks due to the dependency on natural resources and the prevailing high rate of HIV/AIDS.

On 15 March, Finance Minister Saara Kuugongelwa-Amadhila tabled the *national budget*, which was generally viewed in a positive light. For the first time since independence, Namibia's public finances were expected not to end in deficit for a second successive year. Total state income (largely from an estimated N$ 8 bn in taxes from international trade and in particular SACU revenues, as well as a projected N$ 8.7 bn from taxes on income, profits and on goods and services) was projected at N$ 18.3 bn, an increase of 13.4% over 2006. Total planned spending was N$ 17.8 bn, leaving a budget surplus of about N$ 560 m. Capital expenditure increased by almost 40%, totalling N\$ 3.8 bn for 2007–08, while state debt was projected to drop by the end of the fiscal year to N\$ 12.5 bn or 24.7% of GDP (as compared to an estimated 31.3% at the end of the 2006–07 fiscal year). Described as 'pro-poor', the budget made provision for an increase in the annual tax-free income from N\$ 24,000 to N\$ 36,000. Government continued, however, to refuse to institute a Basic Income Grant (BIG) as demanded by a church-led civil society coalition. The main costs remained current expenditure to finance the civil service, with the highest budget allocations going to the educational sector.

In a press release on 16 November, the *IMF staff mission* that conducted the annual article IV consultations attested to the generally favourable economic developments in the country. These, the mission stated, offered "opportunities to strengthen the economic base and reduce poverty". It noted further that high unemployment (officially estimated at more than 35%) called for a larger contribution to growth from non-mineral manufacturing, tourism and other service activities. The natural resource-based economy was indeed a challenge if not curse, since it reinforced the export-orientation and the exploitative nature of the country's economy without creating lasting investment opportunities in employment creation. Local investment in productive sectors was once more one of the unmet challenges, with continued capital transfer abroad.

The appetite for Namibia's raw materials was illustrated by increased external interest in exploiting the country's natural resources, particularly those related to *energy*. The Russian delegation that visited in March along with Prime Minister Fradkov proposed developing a medium-sized nuclear power plant fed by local uranium deposits. It also offered a nuclear-energy production ship to be connected to the national power grid. The Russian Sintez group announced in July that it planned oil drilling operations off the Namibian coast. Mid-year, Brazilian and Japanese investors joined the Chinese and Russians as relative newcomers in exploration activities for uranium, oil and gas. Meanwhile, the pressing

power shortage led to renewed discussions over the potential
exploitation of the Kudu gas field. Growing energy demand resulted
in the decision by cabinet to consider nuclear energy as a potential medium to long-term option. As a shorter-term initiative, the
Caprivi-Link project involving several neighbouring countries was
further pursued towards the end of the year, when two Indian companies were contracted. The project seeks to benefit from the expansion of the Zimbabwean power station at Hwange. Plans to build a
hydropower station at Baynes dam on the Kunene also remained
under discussion.

With the fisheries industry further deteriorating, the *mining
sector* remained the backbone of the country's economic growth
and benefited from soaring world market prices. With the planned
opening of four more uranium mines by 2010, the expected output
will exceed 10% of world production. At the same time, diamond
production by Namdeb, jointly owned by South African mining
giant de Beers and the Namibian government, resulted in increased
profits during the first half of the year. The partners also agreed
in January to extend their partnership until 2013 and to establish
a joint Namibia Diamond Trading Company (NDTC) on an equal
partnership basis for the sorting, selling and marketing of Namdeb
diamonds. Copper, zinc, gold and other precious metals and minerals contributed to the economic stability, which, however, is misleading in terms of overall macroeconomic soundness (as noted
above). Even more clearly, the role of these minerals reflected the
dependency of the economy on a world market, which is currently
enjoying a boom.

Continuing high unemployment and the gross disparities in
income distribution contributed to *growing dissatisfaction* among
ordinary people. The massive presence of foreign interests, not
least in the construction sector in the form of Chinese firms
building large-scale projects under state tenders, resulted for the
first time in public criticism by the National Union of Namibian
Workers (NUNW) which is affiliated with SWAPO and largely loyal to

government policies. In a press conference on 22 November, its secretary general expressed concern over the importation of cheap labour from China for public construction work. He also noted that the Malaysian textile company Ramatex had begun to dismantle some of its machinery, suggesting the imminent closure of its Namibian subsidiary, which had been established with considerable support from the state and the Windhoek municipality as a source of employment for locals. While Namibia continued to enjoy a positive image abroad, increasingly this view was not shared by locals.

Namibia in 2008

The year was dominated by growing polarisation between the governing South West African People's Organisation (SWAPO) and the newly established political opposition, Rally for Democracy and Progress (RDP). Politically motivated acts of violence and an increasingly radicalised rhetoric cast their shadow over the democratic image of the country. Foreign relations remained unspectacular, but Namibia continued to seek closer ties with countries from beyond the Western hemisphere. Food prices and inflation rose markedly and the socioeconomic situation deteriorated towards the end of the year as a result of the global financial and economic crisis. Namibia remained a lower middle-income country with some shocking discrepancies in the distribution of wealth.

Domestic Politics

President Pohamba announced a *cabinet reshuffle* on 8 April, the first since he assumed office three years earlier. While several ministries changed hands and state secretaries were rotated on a large scale, the same old guard was recycled. Former Prime Minister Hage Geingob, who was ousted from office by Pohamba's predecessor Sam Nujoma and subsequently resigned after being demoted to a less prominent portfolio, returned to government after six years as the new minister of trade and industry. His political comeback had been foreshadowed in November 2007 when he was elected deputy president of SWAPO at the party's congress.

Divisions in SWAPO remained visible throughout the year, with the SWAPO Youth League, the Women's League and other branches expressing radical views that contrasted with the gentler approach of President Pohamba. The head of state and party leader, considered to have a conciliatory character, came under repeated internal attack by hardliners for passivity, caution and softness. During politburo and central committee meetings in August, he faced unusually sharp personal attacks and was accused of not consulting with the party before taking decisions in office. These ongoing quarrels fuelled suspicion that influential factions inside the party were seeking to replace Pohamba as the SWAPO candidate for the presidential elections at the end of 2009. Repeated reports in the local media (including the state-owned newspaper) were dismissed as mere speculation, but the ongoing internal differences indicated that power struggles remained the order of the day.

The situation was made more complex by the presence of a *new party*, RDP, itself the result of an internal SWAPO power struggle over the succession to the founding president, Sam Nujoma. Established in late 2007 mainly by former members of the exiled leadership of the liberation movement, it was considered to be the first serious challenge to SWAPO's total dominance. With a leadership home base in the region where the liberation movement originated, RDP claimed to be able to make inroads into the main SWAPO stronghold. These predictions were not confirmed in the first contests, the local elections in the region, where SWAPO maintained its unchallenged dominance, although with a comparatively low voter turnout.

Leaders of the Namibian Lutheran churches responded to the growing polarisation by means of a *pastoral letter* read out during services on 23 March. The four bishops of the three churches expressed the fear that the country was moving backwards in terms of freedom and democracy. The bishops' letter identified "intolerance, verbal and physical attacks and counter attacks" and warned that "failure to redress this situation now can lead to mass loss of lives country wide." The bishops noted that "political opponents are not enemies, but participants in a democratic set-up." This was the first time since independence that the church had commented on politics in such dramatic terms.

The *political rivalries* were radicalised during further contests. On 10 May, SWAPO activists prevented the RDP from holding a political rally, properly registered in compliance with existing laws, in a part of Windhoek's former township Katutura. In condemning this violation of its constitutionally enshrined rights, the RDP released an open letter to President Pohamba, in which it compared this intervention with Hitler's methods and blamed "neo-fascist elements" in SWAPO. The minister of education, in his role as high-ranking SWAPO official, publicly declared shortly thereafter that there would be "no-go areas" for other political parties, since these zones were owned by SWAPO. The RDP responded with a statement branding this as a "fascist inclination". Not surprisingly in light of the year's political escalation, the UN's annual report on 20 August on the Convention on the Elimination of all Forms of Racial Discrimination (CERD), recommended that Namibia review its laws in order to prevent, combat and punish *hate speech*. In its findings, the committee expressed concern that hate speech, mostly by politicians, continued at an unacceptable level and must be stopped.

The *showdown* between SWAPO and the RDP was illustrated by parallel events on 18 October in different parts of Katutura. Some 150 SWAPO supporters tried to prevent a RDP rally at an informal settlement. They refused to follow police orders and were finally dispersed with teargas, while several persons were arrested. The RDP rally was called off. In a political rally held by the SWAPO Party Youth League the same day close by, the Youth League's president demanded that all higher ranking positions in the state apparatus and state-owned enterprises be filled with only reliable SWAPO members and stated, "We have a political religion called SWAPO and the political heaven is SWAPO, and the political hell is where all the other political parties are." As a special guest, the leader of a delegation from the South African ANC Youth League said of the opposition parties: "Destroy these political cockroaches, they are in your kitchen." There was no reaction from the government to this incident. In response to the escalation, all but one smaller opposition party withdrew from the *local by-election* held on 31 October and called for a boycott. Of over 24,000 registered voters, less than

6,000 turned up (22.2%). In earlier elections in this constituency, the number of votes cast exceeded 10,000.

In an unprecedented initiative, founding SWAPO member Andimba Toivo ya Toivo – who was incarcerated for almost 20 years as a political prisoner on Robben Island and later served as a minister in three cabinets until his retirement in 2005 – on 21 November published an open *appeal for tolerance* and respect in the state-owned daily newspaper 'New Era'. He wrote: "We are living in new times that require new ways of conducting political struggle. The formation of new parties and the exchange of differing opinions in the political arena is a normal occurrence in the life of a democracy. The flourishing of new ideas can only contribute to the vitality and development of our nation. The present should be a battle of ideas and not of swords, and the battle should be conducted with respect for our fellow human beings." His was a rare voice of reason within the party establishment.

On 22 November, RDP and SWAPO supporters engaged in *violent clashes* in the north. SWAPO activists again tried to prevent a registered RDP rally, and in the fracas 12 RDP members were reported injured. A deputy minister claimed in a 'New Era' article on 5 December the right of self-defence in response to attacks by political enemies and concluded: "The SWAPO Party shall prevail against the onslaught and all tactics designed by the perpetrators of various methods of violent political abuse ... against our party and its leadership. We the people of Namibia shall win this war, the SWAPO Party shall win this war, and Namibia shall forever remain peaceful."

The new opposition party claimed a small symbolic victory when it secured a high court ruling on the same day (5 December), which granted its urgent application to use the Windhoek College of Education as a venue for the first full RDP *party congress*. The advance booking for the venue had been withdrawn at short notice on the instruction of the permanent secretary of the education ministry. The former foreign minister and SWAPO heavyweight Hidipo Hamutenya was elected unopposed as the party's president.

The position of vice president was also filled with a former SWAPO member while Jesaya Nyamu, a former minister expelled from SWAPO as a result of the earlier power struggle over the Nujoma succession, was elected secretary general. Consequently, in the parliamentary and presidential elections scheduled for the end of 2009 SWAPO will have to compete mainly with former comrades for the electors' votes.

Foreign Affairs

Namibia remained a loyal supporter of the Mugabe government in *Zimbabwe* and fully backed the South African line on negotiations with the regime under siege. Army commander General Martin Shali visited Zimbabwe mid-year for scheduled talks with the military. When this was questioned by some local independent media, the official response was that the visit had been planned long ago and had nothing to do with the political situation. In a rare intervention by local civil society actors, five NGOs on 5 June sent a petition to the head of state urging him to encourage respect for human rights in the neighbouring country. By contrast, an extraordinarily strongly worded editorial in the state owned 'New Era' dismissed what it styled "Botswana's Macho Politics on Zim" and criticised its neighbour's call to close the border as "a declaration of war by other means". On several occasions during the year, the government and president demanded the lifting of sanctions and recognition of the new government, in which ZANU-PF would play a legitimate role and with Mugabe as head of state. This underlined the Namibian commitment to a firm alliance among erstwhile liberation movements in the sub-region, formalised earlier by an internal agreement among MPLA, ZANU-PF, Frelimo, ANC and SWAPO.

Due to these shared views on sub-regional issues, links with *South Africa* became closer. On 5 August, South African President Thabo Mbeki attended the South African-Namibian heads of state economic bilateral commission. Jointly with President Pohamba he inaugurated the first (and South African supported) cardiac unit at the Windhoek central hospital. More importantly, ANC President *Jacob Zuma* twice visited Namibia to cultivate closer ties between the two organisations. After an initial visit on 11/12 August he returned on 8 December to meet with President Pohamba and former President Sam Nujoma. A joint communiqué released by the ANC on 9 December in Windhoek stated "that there is a recurring reactionary debate around the need to reduce the dominance of former liberation movements on the African continent. In this regard the emergence of counter revolutionary forces to reverse the social, political and economical gains that have been made under the leadership of our liberation movements was discussed." In his letter from the president published upon his return in the weekly electronic circular 'ANC Today', Zuma summed up the deliberations thus: "Political analysts and all who claim to know Africans better than they know themselves tell us that it is good for Africa and democracy if the majority of former liberation movements was reduced. How do we as former liberation movements ensure that we do not steer away from our mandate of serving the poor and all our people, in the current climate of counter-revolution?"

Fraternal links were also cultivated with *North Korea*, whose parliamentary chief and political number two Kim Yong Nam paid a state visit on 20–22 March. He attended the independence day celebrations (21 March) and the official inauguration of the new state house. A North Korean construction company had been building the grandiose complex since 2002. The administrative block cost taxpayers over N$ 400 m alone, while the not-yet-completed presidential residence was financed with a N$ 33 m grant from the Chinese government. Another state visit was paid on 13–15 July by the President of *Liberia*, Ellen Johnson-Sirleaf. She addressed parliament and stressed the African bonds of friendship, but made it clear that she considered the Mugabe government an embarrassment.

Relations with the *US* showed some discord. In a letter dated 21 November, 26 of the 50 members of the American house committee on foreign affairs of the US Congress referred to a State Department report showing that in 2007 the US and Namibia had voted in the same way in the UN General Assembly only 7.2% of the time. The committee asked specifically for a policy change on Israel and criticised Namibia as being biased in favour of Palestine. The US embassy declined comment. The prime minister, who acknowledged receipt of the faxed letter but refused to confirm its authenticity, stated that Namibia's policy would remain unchanged. Just a few weeks earlier a dispute had erupted within SWAPO over a motion adopted in parliament to enter into an agreement with the US administration for a $ 305 m Millennium Challenge Account grant for education and tourism projects. It was feared the deal would include preferential access for US investors wishing to establish tourist lodges in the Etosha game reserve and other national parks, to the detriment of local interests in the industry. While the US embassy dismissed the claims, execution of the agreement was put on hold.

Thanks to a proactive and smart ambassador to the *United Nations*, Namibia managed to achieve a high profile and high visibility in General Assembly-related activities. Kaire Mbuende, a former SADC executive secretary and deputy foreign minister, was a near ubiquitous representative who participated in several initiatives.

Socioeconomic Developments

In terms of *financial indicators*, this was a bumpy year for the Namibian economy and consumers. Increased food and fuel prices considerably affected the import-dependent market and resulted in a sharp increase in the inflation rate, which stood at year's end at 10.9% (compared with 7% a year before). With its currency pegged to the South African rand, the Namibian dollar weakened markedly

especially after August and at year's end had depreciated against the
US dollar by 26% (N$ 9.3 to $ 1). While the earlier economic bonanza
enjoyed by the export-oriented economy persisted into the first
part of the year, the latter part witnessed the effects of the global
financial crisis. According to estimates, real GDP growth declined to
around 3% (4.1% in 2007). Deteriorating terms of trade contributed
to a large reduction in the current account surplus. A much higher
fiscal deficit than originally anticipated was expected at the end of
the financial year (March/April 2009).

On 5 March, Finance Minister Saara Kuugongelwa-Amadhila
presented her *annual budget* for 2008–09. She projected average
GDP growth of 5.1% until 2010, which as a result of the global economic crisis proved to be unrealistic. Based on this assumption,
state expenditure was increased to a whopping N$ 22.6 bn, a 26%
increase on the N$ 17.8 bn of the previous fiscal year. At 37.7% of
GDP, it exceeded the target of 30% considerably and in light of the
subsequent economic slowdown could create serious fiscal difficul-
ties. State tax and other revenues were estimated at N$ 20.7 bn, a fig-
ure that will probably also require downward adjustment, thereby
adding to the difficulty of holding the deficit close to the set ceiling,
namely 3% of GDP. Defence spending, unproductive in the context
of Namibia's economy, became the third biggest item, at 10.5% of
total spending (N$ 4.8 bn). According to an analysis by the local
Institute for Public Policy Research, Namibia's military expenditure –
allegedly mainly for infrastructure – amounted to "a far higher proportion than any Western democracy, higher than even the US."

The *mining sector*, the backbone of the economy, experienced a
very mixed year. Rollercoaster commodity prices most affected diamond production and cutting, which had reached an all-time peak
at the beginning of the year only to undergo its biggest collapse
in history by year's end. *Diamond production* by the joint venture
Namdeb (owned by the Namibian state and de Beers) and De Beers
Marine (in charge of the offshore mining) for the first time exceeded
2 m carats. However, lack of sales meant many people had to be laid

off or given early retirement. These developments also affected the diamond cutting and polishing industry established a decade earlier to add value before export, leaving parts of the workforce unemployed. The coastal diamond mining town of Oranjemund, situated in a closed zone to which there is strictly controlled access (the diamond 'Sperrgebiet'), faced a bleak future and increasingly resembled a ghost town. Likewise, the *copper* mine and smelter in the town of Tsumeb closed in December in response to the rapid decline in world prices, which plunged over the year by 65%, from $ 8,000 to $ 3,000 per tonne, and made further production unprofitable. The closure of the mine, which was only a few years earlier celebrated as a success story when it was taken over by the Anglo-Australian multinational Weatherly, left some 600 miners out of work.

Total *investment in mining* was, at N$ 12.7 bn, greater than in any other sector. A German company made the single biggest investment, N$ 2.5 bn in a new cement plant. Despite the mixed results, mining continued to contribute N$ 7.6 bn to the economy, amounting to 12.4% of GDP and over 60% of the total export volume, more than any other sector. Revenue income from mining amounted during the year to N$ 1.6 bn. For the first time since independence, *uranium* contributed more than diamonds to this result. Producing 5,000 tonnes of uranium oxide, Namibia emerged as the fourth biggest producer in the world (after Canada, Kazakhstan and Australia). More open pit mines were licensed and will add to the output, despite growing concerns among environmental groups, who continued in vain to demand more careful environmental impact assessments (the mines, for example, are major consumers of scarce water resources) and better protection from the potentially dangerous activities. The Navachab gold mine near Karibib benefited from the shift by investors to gold as a hedge and the subsequent price of $ 800 per ounce, which contributed to a profitable bottom-line.

A further blow to the economy, adding to the high unemployment rate (estimated at well over 40%), was the final closure of Ramatex.

The last operational unit of the Malaysian *textile company* shut down in early March with the immediate retrenchment of 3,000 workers followed by tense negotiations over compensation, which the company, in violation of Namibian labour law, originally refused to offer. The company also left behind a polluted environment. Ramatex had started production in 2001 mainly for the US market under AGOA after negotiating an attractive investment deal at the expense of the Namibian taxpayer. On balance, almost the only beneficiary of the short-lived bonanza was the foreign company.

A new church and trade union-affiliated initiative was launched for a *Basic Income Grant* (BIG) in the form of a monthly N$ 100 payment by the state to every resident below the age of 60 (when people become eligible for a monthly pension). A pilot project was started in January in an impoverished rural community 100 km east of the capital Windhoek. The initial results were presented by the BIG coalition in September as evidence of success. They were questioned in early November by an economist of a local thinktank, leading to heated controversy, while the government gave no indication it would be willing to consider BIG. Instead, President Pohamba announced before Christmas that political office bearers would receive a 24% salary increase to be implemented in two tranches of 12% during the two consecutive financial years.

Floods in the north (the former Ovamboland) in February caused the displacement of growing numbers of people, estimated in March at over 70,000. 41 people drowned, 11,000 homes were destroyed, as were roads, other infrastructure and large parts of the harvest. The independent National Society for Human Rights, critical of SWAPO, concluded the year on 17 December by presenting a damning human rights report in which it stated that overall human security had deteriorated markedly in all spheres (economic, food, health, environmental, personal and political as well as community security). The official review of *poverty and inequality* in Namibia, published by the Central Bureau of Statistics in October, stated that on the basis of the data from the 2003–04 Namibia household and

expenditure survey, the wealthiest 10% of the country's population (no longer exclusively white) has consumption levels 50 times
higher than the poorest 10%. With a Gini coefficient of 0.63 (a tool
to measure inequality in income distribution among people of a
national economy), inequality is said to have declined but remained
among the highest in the world. As the official report observed, "in
addition to being among the most unequal societies in the world,
Namibia is also among the most polarised." As if this were not bad
enough, the two economists who were the main contributors to the
official report stated in their individual capacities in a separate article that the qualitative data point to deteriorating living conditions.

Namibia in 2009

The year was dominated by domestic politics in preparation for National Assembly and presidential elections held in late November. Despite speculation to the contrary, the former liberation movement, the South West African People's Organisation (SWAPO), maintained its overwhelming dominance over the new Rally for Democracy and Progress (RDP), which had been formed in late 2007 in a break-away move following earlier internal power struggles, and emerged as the official opposition. The election campaign took place in a tense atmosphere and the election results were contested in court. The country's foreign policy continued to shift towards newly emerging partners. The collapse of the diamond industry as a result of the global financial crisis, and reduced income from the customs union, took their toll and contributed to a markedly weaker economic performance.

Domestic Politics

The parliamentary and presidential elections cast their shadow over domestic politics during the year and campaigning for votes was a dominant feature of the local political scene. Faced with growing militancy between party activists, which since 2008 had at times turned political competition and rivalry into a violent affair, the leaders of the Namibian churches issued a "Declaration on Elections" on 31 March. A delegation officially handed a copy to the country's president on 28 April. On 4 June, as a follow-up to this, a church-based steering committee on *churches and elections* in Namibia, appointed on 19 February by church leaders from about 57 different churches and chaired by the former president of the Council of Churches in Namibia, issued an open letter to President Hifikepunye Pohamba and Founding President Sam Nujoma. It expressed concern over

© KONINKLIJKE BRILL NV, LEIDEN, 2016 | DOI 10.1163/9789004321571_008

political statements made towards the end of May by both leaders at different public political rallies and appealed to them to honour the constitutional provisions "so that all of us may go about our daily lawful activities without feeling excluded or being vilified and harassed".

Namibia's first head of state, *Nujoma*, celebrated his 80th birthday (12 May) in the usual style: the Founding Father of the Republic of Namibia (an official title bestowed upon him by parliament when he left State House) appealed to children at a birthday party in a park in Windhoek's city centre to chase away imperialists and colonialists. This militant rhetoric continued with statements at public rallies in his home region in the north. In mid-June, he attacked the Namibian German Evangelical-Lutheran Church for having collaborated with the enemy prior to independence. The church would be tolerated, but any members who asked German friends for help would be shot in the head. Namibian church leaders of several denominations united in the Council of Churches responded by meeting Nujoma on 14 July to share their concerns with the elder statesman. The SWAPO majority dismissed an enquiry by the opposition parties in the National Assembly, since Nujoma was no longer an MP. On 19 September, the founding father, in another speech in the northern region, lashed out against Western imperialism and whites, whom he accused of being as dangerous as black mambas. In a 20 September press release, the National Society for Human Rights (NSHR) quoted Nujoma as saying in his Oshiwambo vernacular: "If you see an English person club (him or her) to the head." During the year, the anything but diplomatic language of the elder statesman also had its impact on the country's foreign relations.

On 22 July, Pohamba announced the suspension of the chief of the *Namibian Defence Force*, Lieutenant General Martin Shalli. He was accused of taking kickbacks dating back to his alleged involvement in arms deals for the Namibian army with Chinese companies while he was ambassador to Zambia, where he had been posted after being relieved of his post as army commander following disagreements with former president Nujoma. When Pohamba took over from Nujoma, he restored Shalli to the highest position in the defence force. The announcement of his suspension came as a bombshell and not only caused unrest within the higher ranks of the army but also provoked intense political speculation as to Pohamba's motives. It was implied that Shalli was the victim of political manoeuvres ahead of the elections. A close ally of former president Nujoma was appointed as acting chief of the defence force.

2 September marked a year since the '*struggle kids*' started public protests demanding compensation for the disadvantages they had suffered as a result of their upbringing in exile. Most of them had been born in Angola. From April, they camped in front of the SWAPO headquarters in Windhoek. On the occasion of the first anniversary of their on-going protest, a large contingent of the 269 members of the group marched to parliament and handed over petitions. They also demonstrated outside the Angolan embassy.

After a long period of waiting, the Electoral Commission of Namibia (ECN) finally announced on 1 September that *parliamentary and presidential elections* would be held on 27 and 28 November. The announcement was preceded by a long period of deliberation around a revised electoral law. For the first time, votes were to be counted and results announced at local polling stations so that sealed ballot boxes would no longer be transported to Windhoek for centralised counting. In addition, the voting period was extended to two days. While the counting at voting stations was welcomed, those afraid of manipulations and vote-rigging criticised the extended voting period, concerned that it might create temptations to manipulate the votes during the second day.

The SWAPO electoral college, whose members were tasked to compile the *list of candidates* for the parliamentary election, took place on 5–6 September. It was preceded by weeks of speculation and positioning. The expected changing of the guard, however, did not ultimately take place. The candidate list offered hardly any surprises or indications of any major political shifts. Likewise, the list of candidates nominated by the RDP on 20 September had few surprises to offer, with no new defectors from SWAPO. Most notably, former minister of agriculture Anton von Wietersheim – a member of the German-speaking minority – attracted most votes from the delegates and was ranked fifth (after the first four places on the list, which were allocated to the party leadership). Like the SWAPO list, the RDP list sought to offer ethnic and cultural pluralism, even though most of the 72 candidates held only symbolic positions, given the likely outcome of the elections.

In October and November, the final stages of the *election campaign* resulted in several violent clashes between the two dominant rival parties, i.e. SWAPO and the RDP. Police at times had to intervene and disperse crowds by using tear gas. Verbal abuse was common, even among leading political office bearers. At a political rally in the harbour town of Lüderitzbucht in mid-November, former prime minister and current minister of trade and industry Hage Geingob accused the RDP of having a "Savimbi syndrome". The RDP protested that this was a form of hate speech.

The first *election results* reported were from the diplomatic missions abroad, surprisingly, before the elections took place in Namibia. While irrelevant in terms of actual numbers, the vote cast in New York, Gaborone and Cape Town indicated a surprisingly high degree of support for the RDP. In response to the result in New York, where SWAPO obtained half of the votes, the leaders of the SWAPO Youth League and the National Union of Namibian Workers demanded at a press conference on 20 November that the head of state recall Namibia's permanent representative to the UN, since the result was considered proof of his disloyalty to the party.

For the first time, the Namibian electorate voted over two consecutive days (27 and 28 November). The reform of the electoral law provided for a count at polling stations in the presence of observers. However, the results were then transmitted to the headquarters of the ECN in Windhoek for final verification before they were officially announced. This resulted in a considerable delay, so that the *official end result* was made known only on 4 December, after days of speculation. Given the relatively small number of votes counted (just over 800,000), this added to the irritation of those already afraid of attempts at manipulation. Beyond all the party arithmetic, which follows below, *women* were the biggest losers. The number of women parliamentary representatives fell from 18 to 16 out of 72, a mere 22% and a far cry from reasonably equal representation.

In spite of these concerns, *election observers* from various African constituencies remained largely satisfied. The SADC observer team recommended a return to polling on a single day in line with the other SADC countries and that equal airtime should be allocated to all parties during the election campaign by the state-owned broadcasting company. The AU observer mission combined its approval of the elections with a reference to "minor problems", which included a "painstakingly slow" counting process. The observer mission of the Pan African Parliament recommended that "the State media in Namibia be insulated from direct Government control by the establishment of an independent media institution" and raised concern over the printing of 1.6 m ballot papers (for a registered electorate markedly below one million) as a potential recipe for vote rigging. Although the mission concluded that the elections took place within the constitutional and legislative framework, it felt that Namibia could do much better.

For the first time in Namibian elections, *local civil society institutions* had formed their own election observation teams. The Namibian Institute for Democracy declared in a statement that it had noted several minor flaws but had not observed any grave irregularities and therefore trusted that the results were by and large credible. The Institute for Public Policy Research, which had created an election watch website, also refrained from any fundamental criticism and seemed largely satisfied that the results reflected the will of the voters. However, the NSHR, generally most critical of the government, was denied observer status after some quarrels with the ECN. Eight of the opposition parties also felt betrayed. They announced in a joint statement on 4 December that they would bring a list of irregularities before the Namibian justice system to *challenge the election results.* On 24 December, the High Court admitted the case.

The results confirmed the *hegemonic status of SWAPO*, with 602,580 votes or 74.3%, thereby retaining 54 of their previously held 55 seats out of 72 seats in parliament. The loss of one seat was anything but a defeat. Some 'pockets' of dissenting votes cast in some of the urban centres and in the central and southern parts of the country were, however, noteworthy. Chief Garoeb's United Democratic Front (UDF) remained the most popular force among the Damara, securing two seats. Chief Riruako drew considerable support for the National Unity Democratic Organisation (NUDO) among the Herero and also took two seats. SWAPO's majority in the southern and eastern regions was reduced. More than ever since the first elections for independence, it again relied on its stronghold in the so-called four O-regions of the former Ovamboland (Oshana, Omusati, Oshikoto and Ohangwena), where for historical reasons it is firmly rooted among more than half of the country's electorate. In these areas, despite the RDP challenge (with its leaders coming from some of these regions), it remained not only by far the biggest, but in most areas still the only, fish in the pond. Even SWAPO – like most of the smaller parties – has some ethnic aspects.

As the *new official opposition*, the RDP, with 90,556 votes (11.16%) and eight seats out of 72, had little reason to celebrate. While it originally boasted of having a database of close to 400,000 supporters, it only attracted 90,556 votes (11.16%). Four of their eight MPs had previously represented SWAPO. The top loser among the *smaller parties* was the Congress of Democrats (CoD), which fell from official opposition status to irrelevant marginality. Two of the small parties' founders managed to survive with one seat each, under flags of the CoD and the newly established All People's Party (APP).

The latter testified to the party's ethnic-regional dimension, with most of its votes secured in the Kavango capital of Rundu. A similar pattern of ethnic-local support characterised the Republican Party (RP) and the Democratic Turnhalle Alliance (DTA), which drew most votes from a white electorate and secured one and two seats respectively. Their declining influence can be seen as indicating the further political marginalisation of the white minority, which was now hardly represented in the National Assembly. The taking of the one seat held by the Monitor Action Group (MAG), the conservative Afrikaans-speaking advocacy group, by the South West African National Union (SWANU), the oldest anti-colonial organisation, was a remarkable symbolic shift.

The results of the *presidential election*, conducted in a parallel ballot with separate ballot papers, showed – as in all previous elections – that the votes for SWAPO's candidate exceeded those for the party. Pohamba received 75.25% of the votes, almost 9,000 votes more than the party list, which underscored his status as a respected leader entrusted by the electorate with running the affairs of the Republic as the head of state, while his new RDP challenger and former comrade Hidipo Hamutenya trailed with 10.91% (88,640 votes). This was a remarkable vote of confidence for Pohamba after a number of internal disputes during his first term in office, when party factions challenged his policy of reconciliation towards some party members accused of being 'unreliable'.

Foreign Affairs

Despite his retirement from political office, former president *Nujoma* remained active and continued to make his mark not only in domestic politics. As the Zimbabwean newspaper 'The Herald' reported, he visited Harare (7–8 July) "to appraise himself on the situation on the ground". Interestingly, this did not make the news in Namibia, though the state media cover the activities of the founding father extensively. This fuelled further speculation about the the identity of the real policy makers behind the scenes. On several occasions at public political rallies, he got carried away making xenophobic statements. Nujoma's explicit reference to the German-speaking minority and their church in Namibia resulted in a *diplomatic note from Germany* seeking an explanation from the foreign ministry. The German parliament discussed the matter on 1 July. Notwithstanding these irritations, Namibian-German bilateral government negotiations on 28–29 July resulted in German financial commitments of € 116.5 m for the next two years. Relations with the *United Kingdom* were also put under strain by one of Nujoma's outbursts during a rally on 19 September. As a result of his insults – he called British and US-Americans and their governments "criminals" – the British High Commission asked the Namibian foreign ministry for an explanation.

Relations with *China* were strained as the result of a series of financial scandals, in which Chinese companies were involved, and by Namibia's decision not to take up a preferential loan offer, which in its view was not really a bargain. Two Chinese news websites, which had reported on the involvement of the Chinese president's son in one of the scandals, were temporarily offline on 21 July and had the news removed. At the end of July, after the Chinese involvement in the Namibian fraud case became international news, the Chinese authorities deleted from search engines all references to 'Namibia' and to the names of the Chinese individuals and companies involved, thus preventing them from being accessed on the Internet and *de facto* eliminating Namibia from the Chinese map of the world.

Some of Namibia's closest allies from the struggle days consolidated friendly relations at the highest levels and also included meetings with Nujoma in their tight schedule. President Dmitry Medvedev of *Russia* arrived for a state visit on 25–26 June, accompanied by a huge delegation, and several agreements were entered into, mainly on economic cooperation, including the involvement of Gazprom in the further exploration and exploitation of the offshore Kudu gas field for local energy production, and Russian participation in the further exploitation of the extensive uranium deposits, even incorporating an option to generate nuclear power.

On 19–20 July, Raul Castro came on a state visit, during which he also met Nujoma, to underline Namibia's friendly relations with *Cuba*. His brother Fidel had never made more than a short stop-over of a few hours, despite Cuba's very prominent role in the final stages of decolonisation, not least through military engagement with the South African army in Angola. Almost 150 Cuban medical doctors and nurses play an essential role in Namibia's public health system, while some 130 Namibian students are studying in Cuba.

Southern African bonds were reinforced on 19 August in the diamond-mining town of Oranjemund, when nine SADC member countries promoted their joint football World Cup-related tourism agenda. The heads of state of Namibia, Zimbabwe and Botswana, as well as the prime ministers of Lesotho and Swaziland, participated in the public relations offensive, which marketed a 'boundless Southern Africa' for visitors to seven transfrontier conservation areas and 30 national parks and nature reserves. Bilateral links with *Botswana* were srengthened at a meeting on 17 August, when delegations led by Namibia's Prime Minister Nahas Angula and Botswana's Vice President Mompati Merafhe met in Windhoek mainly to discuss new infrastructure investments in the Walvis Bay harbour and a railway line to link Botswana with the Namibian port.

At the AU summit in Sirte on 3 July, Namibia was among the countries that endorsed the dismissal of the ICC extradition order for *Sudan's President* al-Bashir. Upon his return, Foreign Minister Hausiku stressed that al-Bashir would be a welcome guest in Namibia. On 9 July, the director of the Legal Assistance Centre, a local human rights agency already active under the South African administration, criticised this as a violation of legally-binding international treaties signed by the government, such as the Treaty of Rome (which established the ICC). He declared that the endorsement of the AU decision suggested that Namibia could not be trusted with its international treaty obligations and was in defiance of its own Constitution, saying: "Considering our recent history of violent oppression under Apartheid, of all nations, we are expected to side with victims of mass murder, rape, mutilation and torture; not with their tyrants and persecutors."

In contrast to the government's dubious stance in solidarity with al-Bashir, the country's permanent representative at the UN, during the UN General Assembly debate at the end of September, vehemently demanded the strict implementation of the AU principle that governments that seized power by means of coups should not be recognised. He led an initiative which ruled on 25 September that the new government of *Madagascar* would not be admitted to participate in the 64th session of the assembly's high-level segment.

Following the state visit by Liberia's President Sirleaf Johnson in 2008, Pohamba reciprocated with a visit to *Liberia* from 28 to 30 July. During a five-day state visit to *India*, Pohamba signed a number of agreements on 30 August, notably for stronger economic cooperation in the diamond polishing sector and with respect to Indian licences for uranium prospecting.

Namibia's international image was damaged by the government's decision to continue with the annual *seal cull* during July. Despite widely organised international protests, the ministry of fisheries granted two seal rights holders a quota of 85,000 seal pups at the seal colonies of Cape Cross and Wolf/Atlas Bay. Two South African journalists who tried to document the cull were arrested and sentenced for contravening the law prohibiting filming without prior permission. Permission was subsequently requested by a local newspaper but was refused. The government's official justification for the criticised practice was that the seals were reducing fish stocks.

Socioeconomic Developments

Major *financial scandals* made headlines during the year. Following investigations by the Anti Corruption Commission, three arrests were made in early July. Those detained included a member of the influential Public Service Commission and a locally resident Chinese businessman, who had links to Nuctech, a Chinese company co-owned by the son of President Hu Jintao. Suspect transactions had allegedly secured the locally based trio over $ 4.3 m for non-existent services after the ministry of finance transferred an advance of $ 12.8 m to the Chinese company in anticipation of the delivery of x-ray equipment for scanning cargo containers and airline baggage. The main costs were to have been covered by a concessional loan from China. On 20 July, Calle Schlettwein, permanent secretary of the finance ministry, confirmed that the government had suspended the $ 100 m credit lines for preferential export buyers credit with the Export-Import (Exim) Bank of China, which had been the main financer of the scanner deal. The reasons given were high interest rates, a tough repayment schedule, the need to limit the purchase of Chinese goods and services, and costly insurance obligations, which made the credit facility unattractive. A *decline in public morale* was reflected in Namibia's further slide on the scale of indicators compiled by the World Bank in its "Doing Business 2010" report released in September. While Namibia had ranked 48th in 2008 and 51st in 2009, it fell to 66th in the prognosis for 2010.

The *annual budget* was presented on 20 March. Finance Minister Saara Kuugongelwa-Amadhila stated that the fiscal tide had turned. The Medium Term Expenditure Framework (MTEF) projections foresaw massive budget deficits for the years to come and an expected increase in the national debt from 20.5% to 29.3% of GDP by the end of the MTEF period in 2011–12. It was estimated that revenue for 2009–10 would fall from N$ 22 bn to N$ 21.8 bn, while total expenditure was increased by 13.1% to N$ 25.4 bn, of which N$ 4.5 bn was allocated to the development budget, an increase of more than half on the previous year. Again, education received the biggest allocation (21.3%), while defence (10.6%) continued to receive more than health (9.5%). The estimated budget deficit was 5.2% of GDP. As a budget analysis of the local Institute for Public Policy Research concluded, renewed international demand for the country's natural resources would be necessary to avoid a national debt crisis and major expenditure cuts in the future.

Diamond production, essentially the country's greatest single source of revenue, suffered major setbacks due to the collapse of the world market. After record sales until mid-2007, production by Namdeb, a joint venture between De Beers and the state, was dramatically cut from the beginning of the year. Shifts were reduced from January to March and a 'production holiday' declared for April to June. Over the first six months of the year, some 400,000 carats were produced, a 60% decline compared with the 1 m carats during the first half of 2008. The government assisted the company, which was confronted with cash flow problems and laid off some 2,000 miners, by permitting it to sidestep the existing diamond trade regulations and sell a significant portion of its stockpile directly to an Indian consortium. This did not prevent Namdeb from ending the year with a net loss of N\$ 414 m in contrast to net profits of N\$ 598 m the previous year. The government provided damage control with a tax breather of N\$ 141 m; the state coffers had received taxes of N\$ 1.4 bn from Namdeb in 2008.

It was expected that increased *uranium* production would compensate for the fall in diamond revenue, but output increased insignificantly compared with the previous year. Namibia nevertheless overtook Russia to end as the fourth biggest uranium producer worldwide with an 11.8% share over the year. In September, new prospecting results for the Rössing South site adjacent to Rio Tinto's big Rössing uranium mine and Paladin's Langer Heinrich suggested that the area ranked among the top five known uranium deposits in the world. This caused some commotion among global players in the uranium mining business and resulted in speculation about who, of the British, Australian, French, Canadian, Chinese, Indian, Russian and other competitors, would manage to secure the investment opportunity to exploit this attractive potential. Government plans to use the uranium resources to embark on *nuclear energy* production were cultivated further through an agreement signed with India on 30 August to seek collaboration in the peaceful uses of nuclear energy. Russia expressed similar interests in collaboration and offered know-how to establish a nuclear energy plant.

During the year, dissonances over the signing of an *interim EPA* increased and the Namibian ministry for trade and industry refused to give in to pressure from Brussels. Together with Angola and South Africa, Namibia did not sign because of unresolved differences. Considerable benefits to the vulnerable, export-oriented economy would be put at risk by the possible loss of preferential access to the EU market. Local producers, especially in the meat sector, which supplied a beef quota to the European market, were concerned about the future.

Namibia in 2010

The year brought the beginning of the second term of office of the head of state and his appointment of an unspectacular new cabinet. 'Business as usual' on the domestic front unfolded, notwithstanding the protracted legal dispute over the parliamentary election results. The results of the communal and regional elections in November confirmed the overwhelming political dominance of the former liberation movement, the South West African Peoples' Organisation (SWAPO), now the SWAPO political party. Ties with China and other Asian countries were further cultivated, while the controversy over the EPAS raged on. The economy managed to recover from the effects of the global financial crisis through increased demand for the country's natural resources (mainly from mining), but poverty reduction and other features of social reality showed less impressive results. Complementing the continued self-enrichment of a new elite and ever-increasing corruption were the serious unemployment rate and the inconclusive debate over a Basic Income Grant (BIG).

Domestic Politics

On occasion of the country's 20th anniversary of Independence on 21 March, President Hifikepunye Pohamba took the oath for his second term of office, and a new cabinet was sworn in. The appointed ministers and their deputies provided few surprises and *party political continuity* was clearly the main intention rather than any spectacular changes. While some of the old guard retired or were phased out, the few members of the younger generation who entered the higher-ranking echelons had little influence as yet. Despite earlier noble declarations, women's representation in parliament and cabinet declined to less than a quarter. The new constellation provided no clues as the answer to the overriding question of who would have the best chances in positioning her/himself for the next elections at the party congress in 2012, which would be decisive for the choice of the party's next presidential candidate. Below the surface, a long drawn-out power struggle had started within the party and its sub-organisations, which fueled rumours and speculation throughout the year as to who had the best chance in the race.

The protracted court case over the *disputed 2009 parliamentary election results* continued throughout the year without any conclusive result. On 4 March, the High Court dismissed the application by nine opposition parties on purely formal grounds. An appeal to the Supreme Court resulted in a decision on 6 September to set aside the original ruling, on equally technical grounds, and to re-admit the case. Matters were pending at year's end, while the eight elected members of the official opposition party, Rally for Democracy and Progress (RDP), boycotted the swearing in and refused to take their seats while the verdict was pending. They only joined the national assembly on 14 September, amidst first controversial exchanges in a tense atmosphere.

SWAPO dominance was underscored by the results of the *regional and local authority elections* of 26 and 27 November. A disappointing turn out of 38.6% of registered voters did not dampen SWAPO's elation at clenching absolute majorities in all but one of the 13 regional councils. Out of a total of 107 constituencies in the 13 regions, SWAPO captured 97. Results for all other parties except the RDP, which got its best results in urban constituencies, once again testified to their regional-ethnic appeal, with limited local community strongholds. The only substantially dissenting vote was in the north-eastern Kunene region, where the regional council had a non-SWAPO majority. The party secured 226 seats in a total of 50 local authorities, with the RDP trailing behind with 48 elected candidates on 36 local councils.

SWAPO's firm political control over the country was further entrenched through a highly controversial amendment of the act regulating the election of *regional governors*. Nominated from among the elected regional councillors, governors were now to be appointed by the head of state and did not have to be elected. The newly adopted Special Advisors and Regional Governors Appointment Act, which was pushed through parliament in October, allowed for appointments that did not reflect the political majority in the region. As a result, even the Kunene region, with a non-SWAPO majority, was now represented by a SWAPO governor. The new understanding was that governors "should be appointed by the President as the representatives of the constitutional head in the various regions" and that they "should not be one of the regional councilors. This mode of appointment would strengthen the unitary nature of the state, and make positive contribution to the concept of taking government to the people", as Trade Minister Hage Geingob argued in his address in parliament on 6 October. This made it seem that people were no longer entitled to take their views to government. Despite this dubious concept of democracy, the Mo Ibrahim Index released in early October once again ranked Namibia 6th out of 53 countries on the continent in terms of good governance.

Foreign Affairs

The newly appointed *Foreign Minister* Utoni Nujoma (a son of the former president and SWAPO leader Sam Nujoma) was among the surprise appointments to cabinet, since he had no expertise in this area. Through his first nine months in office, he seemed to carefully avoid any signs of incompetence and – in contrast to his earlier performances as deputy minister of justice – maintained a low profile in terms of public statements.

The annual SADC summit took place in Windhoek on 16–17 August, with all 15 member countries' heads of state in attendance. In the midst of the celebrations of the sub-regional grouping's 30th anniversary, Pohamba took over the annual chairmanship. Namibia was no controversial sub-regional player and maintained an unspectacular low profile in most foreign policy matters. The centenary of *SACU* as the world's oldest customs union was celebrated on 22 April at its headquarters in Windhoek. A conflict between the member countries emerged from discussions over a modified revenue sharing formula. Namibia criticized the South African initiative, which would cause major declines in revenue income for the smaller economies.

Ties with friends from the 'struggle days' were cultivated further. A state visit by Pohamba to *Russia* resulted in three agreements on fisheries, tourism and education. A government-owned potential new uranium mine was linked with the Russian State Atomic Energy Corporation when, on 20 May, Presidents Pohamba and Medvedev signed a memorandum of understanding that committed Russia to an investment of over $1 bn in uranium exploration and production over five years (renewable) to feed with Namibian uranium a still-to-be-constructed Russian-owned nuclear power station in Turkey. The National Aluminium Company, the largest state-owned company in *India*, announced in September plans to investigate the possibility of using Namibian uranium for a nuclear power plant in India.

Namibia's *uranium deposits* were a sensitive factor in international policy. In late January, a US initiative sought to minimise risks of the illegal sale of Namibian uranium after police had arrested in September 2009 three people who had tried to sell 170 kg of stolen uranium oxide. Iran's 15% stake in the Rössing uranium mine operated by Rio Tinto, held since 1975, was also a matter of concern. On 9 June, the UNSC adopted resolution 1929, which imposed new sanctions on Iran and included restrictions on investment in uranium mines. Following talks with the governments of the US, the UK, Australia and Namibia, London-based Rio Tinto declared on 27 October that the existing ownership was in compliance and that any future Iranian shareholder expansion would revert to the Namibian government, which held a 3% share in the mine. In 2009,

Rössing sold 46% of its output to Asian, 32% to North American, 11% to European and 11% to Japanese power utilities. *Wikileaks* disclosed in early 2011 a US cable dated 26 February 2009 and sent to embassies in London and Canberra, which expressed concern that Iran might try to obtain uranium from Namibia. The cable urged that assurances be obtained from both Rio Tinto and the Namibian government that no uranium supplies would be delivered to Iran.

Germany remained the biggest single donor to Namibia, despite German institutions being publicly criticised for undue interference in Namibian affairs. In response to a critical report, published by the German Africa Foundation, on the parliamentary and presidential elections of November 2009, which was based on the analyses of election observers who had toured the country with the assistance of the local office of the Konrad Adenauer Foundation (KAS), Prime Minister Nahas Angula alleged on 17 February that these institutions had the ulterior motive of accelerating regime change and had abused Namibian hospitality. A statement by the SWAPO Party Youth League had already called upon government in late January to expel the KAS representative and, following these allegations, the resident representative of the KAS was declared a threat to political stability. The president of the national trade union umbrella body affiliated to SWAPO declared on 19 February that Germans could "go to hell" if they interfered with Namibian politics. He furthermore linked the controversy to a three-day visit by Germany's Minister for Development Cooperation Dirk Niebel in early February, calling him "arrogant and provocative" for his defence of the German institutions in an interview with the state owned newspaper 'New Era'. These skirmishes remained a storm in a teacup and were not followed by any official démarche, but they testified to the strong negative sentiments that existed with regard to the former colonial power. These flared up again when, in September, a Namibian minister, in transit at Munich airport (returning from an UN conference in Mexico), was suspected of carrying a forged passport and interrogated. He missed his connecting flight and the incident resulted in a brawl during which the minister exchanged heated words. On 14 September, 'New Era' quoted him as accusing the German officials of an attitude like that exhibited when they "massacred and committed genocide here", and of behaving "like neo-Nazis and neo-Hitler's [sic]".

Support from *donor partners* in the fiscal year 2010/11 was estimated to amount to N$ 265 m through the State Revenue Fund and N$ 2.2 bn outside the State Revenue Fund, constituting 9% of annual expenditure. Notwithstanding the importance of the EU as a massive contributor to Namibia's developmental projects, Trade Minister Geingob challenged the EU over the unfair implications of the *Interim EPA* (IEPA), which he refused to sign. On 19 May in the Namibian parliament, he explained that he had refused, despite open threats by the EU, because it might result in painful losses for Namibian exports to the EU market. Among the serious economic and policy consequences he listed were that the IEPA would lead to the need "to forfeit the policy option of using export taxes on raw materials as an important incentive for value addition", and to abandon the current system of infant industry protection and the loss of investments in horticultural marketing, grain storage, agricultural extension and value addition to food products, which "would seriously disrupt rural economies and the livelihoods of thousands of small farmers". Another bone of contention remained the Most Favoured Nations clause, since the IEPA, stipulated that all trade agreements entered into with parties holding above 1.5% of global trade automatically entitled the EU to the same preferences. In the light of a trade agreement negotiated between SADC and India, this was considered an obstruction to the desired strengthening of South-South trade relations.

Friendly relations with Asian partners notably *China*, were also visible in the trade exchanges. Namibia had a positive trade balance due to the export of its raw materials (mainly minerals). In March, the chairman of the Chinese People's Political Consultative

Conference and the vice-minister of foreign affairs undertook diplomatic consultations in Namibia, while former president Nujoma and Trade Minister Geingob attended the Shanghai World Expo on different occasions. Wikileaks caused some irritation by disclosing in December the claim by foreign diplomats that Namibia had allowed the resettlement of 5,000 Chinese families in the country in compensation for a loan on which it had defaulted. This was dismissed by Prime Minister Angula on 15 December as "unsubstantiated and mere fabrications", but it fueled already existing suspicions that the Chinese received preferential treatment over and above anyone else.

Socioeconomic Developments

In September, the *IMF* published its staff report on the 2010 article IV consultation, which ended on 26 May. It praised the government for a countercyclical policy stance, which, through increased expenditure, cushioned the impact of the global crisis. On the flip side, this created a projected fiscal deficit of over 8% of GDP, leading to a rapid accumulation of public debt, which resulted in an increased public debt-to-GDP ratio of almost 20% (up from almost 15%). The report also admitted that, "despite the strong macroeconomic performance, Namibia's key social indicators remain weak" – a mild euphemism for the stark discrepancies displayed in social realities, which ranked the country (statistically in the middle-income category) at the top of the Gini-coefficient (measuring the skewed distribution of wealth in terms of income inequality).

Namibia once again scored well in its *performance ranking* in comparison with other sub-Saharan African countries. According to the World Economic Forum's Global Competitiveness Index released on 9 September, Namibia ranked as the 74th most competitive country out of 139. This confirmed the modestly positive trend. The 2010 Index of Economic Freedom, also published in September, and compiled by the 'Wall Street Journal' and the Heritage Foundation, ranked Namibia 77th out of 183 countries and classified it as 'moderately free'. The international applause stemmed from rather conservative quarters and was probably not shared by many among the ordinary locals on the receiving end, in the light of some of the socioeconomic realities.

In contrast to the relatively good marks with regard to economic freedom, *corruption* (which could be considered somewhat cynically as an integral part of 'economic freedom') was considered 'significant'. This was reflected in the graft ladder provided on 26 October by TI, whose Corruption Perceptions Index indicated that the country was perceived as 'highly corrupt' and ranked 56th out of 178 countries. Recent years have shown a remarkable decline compared with the rankings a decade earlier, when Namibia was among the top 30 least corrupt countries. During the year, poor deals made by the Government Institution Pension Fund (GIPF) under its Development Capital Portfolio during previous years were in the headlines and were the subject of much infuriated public debate after it became known that, as a result of earlier disbursements of N$ 950 m to local companies owned by well-connected individuals, some N$ 660 m were subsequently written off as bad debts. What added to the public outcry was the government's failure to actively deal with the matter or to take the GIPF officials to task, but rather to keep any investigations locked away and to shelve the issue. The report of an internal investigation by a South African firm of accountants and auditors, which was kept secret, revealed massive irregularities in the disbursement procedures. As 'New Era' reported on 13 September, the document detailed how companies that received loans where owned by people "who seemingly, had no business acumen other than access to funds". Some start-up companies "received funds without submitting loan applications to the GIPF or business plans". Other loans were awarded "to companies found to be in technical insolvent state, while numbers were flipped around to boost up the total loan value above the requested amount." Growing

evidence released over the year through the local media documented mind-boggling embezzlement on a grand scale, which
involved high-ranking office bearers in Namibian institutions.
The disclosure by the local monthly journal 'Insight' in April that
Namibian members of parliament – in gross violation of the laws
adopted by them – had not fully disclosed their assets and liabilities
since 2003, did not, therefore, come as a surprise.

In contrast to the above kind of 'self-help schemes', most
Namibians were less privileged and lacked access to any meaningful financial income. On 27 September, the government announced
the results of the 2008 Namibia Labour Force Survey, which confirmed an *unemployment* rate of 51.2% among the economically
active population. Those aged 15 to 24 years were the most affected
group. A drastic decline in the agricultural sector was attributed
to the negative effects of climate change, the global economic
crisis and the closure of mining operations. The local *construction
industry*, however, lamented the negative effects of awarding the
most attractive public works tenders to foreign (mainly Chinese
and North Korean) construction companies, which left the local
industry ailing and resulted in redundancies for Namibian workers. They bemoaned the fact that Chinese bids (suspected of being
subsidised by the Chinese government) undercut local offers at
the expense of investment in Namibian capacity and work places,
while often violating Namibian labour legislation.

The achievements of *land reform*, whose declared policy aim
was to provide opportunities for income generating activities
among hitherto landless people, once again fell far below expectations. A report presented by the Legal Assistance Centre on
12 September confirmed suspicions that beneficiaries were not
necessarily the needy, but those with political connections, and that
criteria were often ignored or by-passed to the advantage of people
in privileged positions. Commenting on a new *land bill* released for
public consultation, a review published by the local Institute for
Public Policy Research bemoaned the reduced accountability and

transparency in terms of land allocation. In view of emerging 'land grabs', it warned that "people in communal areas will be vulnerable to the predations of international investors and their local allies".

The *annual budget* for 2010/11 was presented by Finance Minister Saara Kuugongelwa-Amadhila on 30 March. As noted above, the expenditure reflected an expansionary approach to counteract the economic decline that had resulted from the global financial crisis. The record volume of N\$ 27.6 bn (excluding statutory expenditure) translated into a budget deficit exceeding 7%. Education again received the biggest share, with N\$ 6.47 bn (22.4%), an increase of 20.5%. N\$ 3.96 bn were allocated to the ministry of finance, of which N\$ 1.3 bn was to service state debt. The ministry was also set to inject more than half a billion Namibia dollars into various state-owned enterprises – including N\$ 80 m in bail-outs to Air Namibia, N\$ 83.9 m to TransNamib, N\$ 100 m to the public energy utility NamPower, N\$ 100 m to the Road Fund Administration, N\$ 60 m to the Agricultural Bank of Namibia and N\$ 50 m to NamWater and the Development Bank of Namibia. N\$ 3 bn were allocated to the defence ministry – an increase of 16%, amounting to 10.4% of the total budget. The ministry of health and social services received N\$ 2.59 bn, compared with N\$ 2.4 bn in 2009. As a commentator critically remarked, for every Namibian dollar Namibian taxpayers spent on a nurse, they spent N\$ 1.6 on a soldier. He reminded the audience at a traditional breakfast debate with the finance minister after the budget was tabled, that, a decade earlier, defence spending amounted to 7.3% of expenditure, less than half the amount for health expenditure.

Revenue was projected to follow a downward trend, being down 8.9% at N\$ 22.536 bn. *SACU revenue shocks*, predicted for 15 years, now became a reality. Following a long-awaited initiative, South Africa started to question the revenue sharing formula as too beneficial for the smaller economies. For Namibia, the decline in revenue income was expected to be around 30% and more than 50% in the following year, partly because of a fall in income to the revenue pool as a result of trade liberalisation with the bigger trading partners and subsequent tariff reductions.

Being one of only three countries in sub-Saharan Africa that provided its citizens with social safety nets by means of an old-age pension and other social payments, the discussion over the *introduction of a BIG* became increasingly heated. Initiated as a pilot project for the residents in a village by a church-led BIG coalition, every member of the community had received N$ 100 per month. As the BIG coalition argued, the results justified the investment and suggested that government introduce a countrywide BIG. On 27 April, answering a question following his State of the Nation address in parliament, Pohamba dismissed the demand for a BIG, saying it was a form of exploitation of those who earned their living working for a salary, while their taxes would be used as pay-outs for others. The president of the SWAPO-affiliated National Union of Namibian Workers (NUNW) subsequently announced in early July, that it had abandoned the BIG coalition. Delegates at the NUNW's national congress at the beginning of September, however, passed a resolution tasking the newly elected leadership to re-join the BIG coalition as a meaningful effort to reduce poverty among Namibia's most destitute population.

The mining sector remained the backbone of the economy, and the year registered an increase in most prices and sales. It was estimated that the operations of a total of 19 exploration and mining companies contributed jointly to around 12% of GDP. The *diamond* company Namdeb (jointly owned by de Beers and the Namibian state) reported an increased production of 1.475 m carats, 57% above the previous year (940,000 carats). After an earlier decrease in sales, a total of 1.52 m carats were sold, an increase of 11.6%. Thanks to higher world market prices, the income of N$ 5.58 bn was markedly above the N$ 3.81 bn of the previous year. According to information provided by the Kimberley Process Certification Scheme, Namibian diamonds scored on average by far the highest prices worldwide ($ 343) per carat.

Uranium production also gained momentum towards year's end. Namibia was the world's fourth biggest producer of yellow cake, with around 10% of the world's production. Over 60 mostly foreign companies held exclusive exploration licenses. In the absence of a policy framework, government had decided on a moratorium in 2007. Four companies had mining licenses with two mines in operation and two under construction. The sites run by Paladin Energy for the Langer Heinrich mine (operational since 2007) and the Rio Tinto group for the Rössing mine (operational since 1976) produced around 5,279 tonnes of yellow cake, slightly less than the previous year (5,429 tonnes), but with a markedly higher spot price on the world market, almost doubling over the year. A process of establishing a legal framework for the regulation of uranium mining was initiated towards the end of the year by the ministry of mines, as the Minerals Act lacked provisions to meet the statutory obligations and international standards pertaining to uranium. On 29 November, a stakeholders' conference discussed exploration, mining and milling policy, as well as *nuclear energy*. Minister Katali reiterated at the meeting earlier policy announcements that government planned to utilise the uranium resources to develop a nuclear power plant. The country would also explore options for the local storage of nuclear waste.

A major deal in the mining sector was announced in early December with the take-over of the Skorpion *zinc* mine at Rosh Pinah from Anglo American by the Indian based mining company Sterlite Industries at a price of $ 707 m. Skorpion Zinc was the world's eighth biggest producer with a designed annual capacity of 150,000 tonnes, with a value of $ 236 m in 2009. The new owners, in a move to become the world's top producer of integrated zinc and lead products, declared their intention to extend the life span of the mine (currently until 2016) and its production capacity. In 2009, the mine had contributed 2.5% of Namibia's GDP.

Namibia's *younger generation* faced a bleak future. According to the UNAIDS report for 2010, HIV prevalence among Namibian youths aged 15 to 24 declined from more than 10% in 2007 to about 5% in 2009. A report by the National Planning Commission on the situation of children and adolescents presented in early December revealed, in contrast, a sobering picture: infant mortality rose again (one out of every 15 children died before the age of five), about 40% of rape victims were estimated to be children, up to 80% of children were undernourished, and many primary school learners experienced hunger and neglect. On the other hand, 90% of 6- to 12-year-olds were enrolled in primary schooling. On 9 March, a report was tabled in parliament that addressed the growing social problem of baby dumping or infanticide as "a significant one", and at a workshop at the end of April a representative of the ministry of health and social services maintained that every third woman in the country was a victim of domestic violence.

Approaching the 20th anniversary of Namibian Independence, Prime Minister Angula suggested at a public lecture on 2 March that, "...a cup may be half full or half empty. We are not likely to agree with the level of progress we are making." He declared the youth challenge to be a national challenge and warned of a "point when young people suffering from poverty and unemployment will say enough is enough". According to him, the question was whether progress over the first 20 years had been sufficient.

Namibia in 2011

The contest for the up-coming head of state elections emerged as a prominent political feature during the year, which in terms of domestic politics presented no surprises. The results of the 2009 parliamentary elections continued to be contested in a prolonged legal battle. Poverty remained a challenge and the government responded to the high unemployment rate by introducing a new three-year capital investment programme. Despite the lack of visible socioeconomic progress and increased signs of corruption, political stability was maintained. International relations continued to favour new friends over old ties, with the EPA remaining contested and bilateral relations with Germany still tested by memories of the genocide committed more than a century ago.

Domestic Politics

The *disputed elections* for the National Assembly that took place at the end of November 2009 kept the legal system busy. On 14 February, the High Court dismissed for lack of substantial evidence allegations of electoral fraud initiated by nine opposition parties. The ruling SWAPO party, however, expressed strong concern over the verdict that the Electoral Commission had failed to maintain a satisfactory state of affairs in organising the elections. On 9 March, the applicants stated their intention to appeal to the Supreme Court against the judgment, but failed to provide evidence to the registrar within the stipulated three months. Judgment in the matter of the appeal was scheduled for 5 October, when the Supreme Court only announced that the merits of the case would be considered at a later stage. At year's end, the legal wrangles had been taking place for over two years without a final settlement.

© KONINKLIJKE BRILL NV, LEIDEN, 2016 | DOI 10.1163/9789004321571_010

Meanwhile, it was more or less business as usual as far as politics were concerned, with no initiatives by *opposition parties* significant enough to challenge the dominance of the SWAPO party (previously: South West African Peoples Organisation). Given the mediocre level of the challenge represented by the political opposition, often more engaged in internal squabbles than in representing meaningful alternatives, the former liberation movement's de facto one-party rule was not at risk. Hence, policy debates within SWAPO and with its affiliated allies such as the National Union of Namibian Workers remained of more interest than any other political discussions.

The *race for the presidency*, with elections due in late 2014 and the new incumbent's term of office to run from March 2015, unfolded with two prominent contestants in the arena. Minister of Trade and Industry Hage Geingob (the former prime minister) and Minister of Justice Pendukeni Iivula-Ithana – the party's deputy president and secretary general respectively – emerged as the most obvious and ambitious candidates. Their early campaigns got under way despite repeated denials and some public speculation about possible factionalism. This prompted Hifikepunye Pohamba, the party president and head of state, to intervene at the party's central committee meeting on 19 November. He appointed a team to investigate allegations of smear campaigns between the two frontrunners, whom he cirticised for divisive politics and creating bad blood in the party. Other potential candidates to succeed him were the party stalwart, Lands Minister Jerry Ekandjo, and Foreign Minister Utoni Nujoma, son of the first head of state. Pohamba warned against the fomenting of tensions similar to those that had arisen during his nomination as presidential candidate in 2004, which resulted in the break-away of a SWAPO faction and the establishment of the new Rally for Democracy and Progress, which became the official opposition.

According to the Mo Ibrahim Foundation's *good governance* index, released in early October, Namibia ranked 6 out of 53 African countries. The Foundation observed, however, that during the previous five years (2006 to 2010) the standard of governance in the country had worsened. The controversy surrounding the repatriation of skulls from Germany in memory of the genocide more than a century earlier (see more details below) culminated in a *spectacular public outburst* by Minister of Youth, National Service, Sport and Culture Kazenambo Kazenambo, who had been the head of the delegation charged with repatriating the skulls. In response to criticism of excessive expenses incurred to fund a large delegation, published in a local newspaper on 11 November, he called a press conference on 16 November, where, enraged over the issue, he lambasted the newspaper that had carried the report, called the journalist a "bloody *boer*" with former links to the South African army, and threatened that black Namibians' patience with the colonial mentality that surfaced in such criticism was running out. With reference to the continued disproportionately high ownership of land by commercial white farmers, he suggested that the constitution could be set aside if the whites were to "scratch too far". Most of the media and parts of the local community reacted strongly to this apparent lack of diplomacy, but seemed to underestimate the event as an indicator of the growing frustration. The minister's outburst was an over-reaction to the insensitive self-righteousness often displayed by a privileged minority, but it is ignorance of the feelings of the formerly colonised majority that should be seen as a root cause of such displays of emotion. Given the continued scandalous discrepancies between the haves and the have-nots, as well as the minister's humiliating experience during his visit to Germany, when he was refused any meeting at ministerial-level and a state secretary left the only official ceremony after delivering her statement, this outburst should be seen in the context of the lack of progress with regard to national reconciliation.

The year was marked by a public outcry over the fact that hundreds of destitute people of all ages survived by regularly waiting for food that had exceeded its sell-by date to be delivered to the dumping grounds outside Windhoek and other towns. When policy makers pleaded ignorance of this shocking reality, they were accused by the local media of being out of touch. *Poverty* continued to be widespread. According to World Bank statistics, Namibia ranked as the higher-middle-income country with the highest level of poverty in the world. Poverty and unemployment were also considered as root causes of the high suicide rates, especially in the rural northern region, and of a dramatic rate of infant abandonment and infanticide. The director general of the National Planning Commission (NPC) announced on 23 November that the gap between the haves and have-nots was higher in 2009/10 than in 1993/94. The government continued, nonetheless, to dismiss any demands for the introduction of a Basic Income Grant (BIG), promoted for a few years by a local civil society alliance.

In striking contrast, in the course of the year the government purchased a new fleet of Mercedes Benz cars for top ranking officials and a new jet and two state-of-the-art S600L Mercedes Benzes for the president, while a battery of E-Class Mercs remained on the shopping list for ministers and deputy ministers. The leaders of the SWAPO Youth League openly criticised the shopping spree in mid-October as *misplaced priorities*. The frustration of ordinary people over the failure of their elected leaders to deliver measures to ease their struggle for survival could emerge as a greater political challenge for SWAPO in the years to come than any organised political opposition.

Foreign Affairs

The absence of any coherent foreign policy was ridiculed on 2 December in a weekly editorial by the former editor of the most widely read independent daily newspaper, 'The Namibian'. In fact, the former president's son, Utoni Nujoma, who had been foreign minister for two years, did not, contrary to all expectations, use this influential ministerial position to enhance his own profile by formulating a foreign policy concept of his own making. While bilateral relations were promoted through *state visits* by Finland's President Tarja Halonen (22 February) and President John Atta Mills of Ghana (25–28 August), foreign policy continued to reflect increasingly friendly relations with countries such as China, Iran and North Korea without any clearly indicated systematic strategy.

The situation in *Libya* revived the struggle mentality of yesteryear, and the intervention sanctioned by the UNSC was criticised both by members of the government and by leaders of SWAPO as an imperialist conspiracy for regime change. In his speech on Namibia's 21st Independence Day on 21 March, President Pohamba condemned the intervention "in the strongest terms", saying: "Our brothers and sisters in Libya are under attack from foreign forces." Former president Nujoma added the same week that this was a "crime against humanity" and a violation of international law. On 11 July, Minister of Justice Pendukeni Ithana confirmed that Namibia would not comply with the ICC arrest warrants for Kadhafi and Sudanese President Omar al-Bashir. Namibia was among the 22 countries that objected in the UN General Assembly on 16 September to accepting the National Transitional Council as the body officially representing Libya. On 23 September, Pohamba declared in his speech at the 66th session of the General Assembly that the intervention in Libya was reminiscent "of the infamous Berlin Conference of 1884/1885, when Africa was carved up by imperial powers".

Zimbabwe's Prime Minister Morgan Tsvangirai visited Windhoek on 28 March to meet Pohamba as head of *SADC* in order to lobby for his party's position on Zimbabwean politics. Despite his office in the government of national unity, the leader of the Movement for Democratic Change was reportedly given the cold shoulder, as in all previous years. In early August, Windhoek hosted leading representatives from another five *former liberation movements* now in political control as governments in Angola, Mozambique, South Africa, Tanzania and Zimbabwe. The final summit on 11 August was preceded by consultative meetings between the youth wing leaders and the secretaries general of the parties. Agreement was reached that such meetings should take place as side events at every SADC summit to strengthen relationships.

An official visit to *Iran* by Foreign Minister Nujoma and Mines and Energy Minister Katali in December underlined the friendly relations between the two countries. It was announced that an Iranian embassy would soon be established and that Iran had decided to invest in an oil refinery in Namibia. This would replace an earlier agreement signed with Nigeria.

During the first nine months of the year, almost 2,000 Namibians applied for *asylum in Canada*, the third highest number of applicants after China and Hungary. Namibians did not require a visa to enter Canada, but in December the Canadian government alerted Air Namibia that Namibians would be scrutinised more closely if they did not have proper travel documents and meet the appropriate entry requirements. According to the local human rights body NamRights, human trafficking was a main reason for Namibians being stranded in Canada, while others were seeking asylum for their links to the Caprivi secessionist movement, which had been prosecuted by the state for high treason.

Bilateral *relations with Germany* remained contested, even though the former colonial power continued to be the biggest single donor country and despite the fact that German Minister for Development Cooperation Dirk Niebel visited the country at the end of August for the second time within 19 months. Early October witnessed the first repatriation of skulls from Germany. They were remains and reminders of the genocide committed by the German colonial army in 1904–1908 and had been taken to Germany for anatomical measurement In line with the Arian obsession with categorising variations between human beings. The visit of a delegation of Herero and Nama descendants to transfer the skulls of their ancestors culminated in a diplomatic wrangle over how to bring about reconciliation with the past. This sensitive issue was exacerbated by *demands for reparation* by the most affected communities, who felt their case had not been adequately recognised. Germany's ambassador to Namibia added fuel to the flames when he suggested, at the signing on 16 November of a new cooperation agreement worth over N\$ 660 m, that the Namibian delegation had visited Germany with a hidden agenda and had created a negative impression of bilateral relations between the two countries. Enquiries by opposition parties in the German parliament, as well as a public debate in Namibia and Germany, illustrated the dissonances, also documented in the ministerial outburst reported above.

On 13 September, *EU* Trade Commissioner Karel de Gucht, while on a trip to Southern Africa, met in Windhoek with Pohamba, other ministers and representatives of the trade and business world in an effort to promote the conclusion of an EPA. The meeting ended with no concrete results and the deadlock over unresolved matters continued, while de Gucht made no reference to an ultimatum for the signing of an EPA announced only two weeks later by Brussels.

Socioeconomic Developments

Finance Minister Saara Kuugongelwa-Amadhila tabled the *annual budget* for 2011/12 on 9 March, projecting record expenditure of almost N\$ 38 bn, of which N\$ 35.8 bn was domestic government expenditure (an increase of 30% on the previous year), with more than N\$ 2 bn additional interest costs to service government debt. With estimated revenue of N\$ 28 bn, an unprecedented 9.8% GDP deficit was anticipated. This brought the overall debt ratio close to 30% of GDP. The inflated size of new debts took local economists by surprise and resulted in a controversial debate over whether to prioritise fiscal prudence or social investment. The highest allocations were to the ministries of education (N\$ 8.3 bn), finance (N\$ 3.65 bn), health and social services (N\$ 3.3 bn) and defence (N\$ 3.1 bn), and totalled over 50% of planned expenditure. The addition of allocations to the ministries of justice, administration, safety and security brought this to 80%, including allocations of N$ 2 bn for the police and N$ 1.2 bn for war veterans. The remaining 20% was allocated to the economic ministries (mines, trade, land, agriculture, fisheries, transport, tourism and planning).

The main budget increase came from the introduction of a Targeted Intervention Programme for Employment and Economic Growth (TIPEEG) with total investments of N$ 14.6 bn over three years for job creation. On the basis of a 2007/8 survey by the ministry of labour, the *unemployment* rate in 2010 was estimated at over 51%. While this figure remained contested, economists agreed that the TIPEEG seemed not to be based on any realistic assessments. Investments through the development budget for the next three years were intended to create over 180,000 jobs in the private sector and public works, but there was little efficient implementation during the rest of the year, due not least to a lack of capacity. On 19 August, Pohamba summoned four ministers to State House to account for the lack of progress. At the end of its yearly mission, which took place from 9 to 22 November, an IMF delegation cautioned that reliance on a TIPEEG would not be enough to combat unemployment.

In contrast to the claim that the budget was pro-poor, no tax adjustments benefited low-income groups, and income *inequality* continued unabated. As observers noted, rising government expenditure over the 20 years since independence had not translated into job creation, reduction of poverty or less income discrepancy. At the end of August, the BIG coalition expressed disappointment over the government's ultimate withdrawal of the planned introduction of a levy on the export of raw materials. The tax reform was shelved after intensive lobbying by the mining industry. The BIG coalition pointed out that the continued zero-rating on the export of *raw materials* gave a free tax ride to those who extracted natural resources.

On 1 December, TI released its latest Corruption Perceptions Index, according to which the country maintained its score of 4.4, and remained in the category of *highly corrupt* although its overall ranking was 57th least corrupt out of 183 economies and second least corrupt in the region – which showed that everything is somewhat relative. A World Bank study presented towards year's end focused on money laundering in Malawi and Namibia. It suggested that government corruption in Namibia was a bigger problem than other forms of organised crime and fraud. Tax evasion was estimated at 9% of GDP and by far the largest source of ill-gotten money. Dubious foreign investments also affected the property market. A considerable cash inflow from Angola was used for the purchase of land and estates, contributing to a boom, fuelled to a large extent by money laundering activities.

Another worrying tendency was the ballooning of *tender exemptions* for public works. A report presented by the Institute for Public Policy Research (IPPR) on 9 September documented that exemptions from normal tender procedures had become the rule, bypassing scrutiny by the tender board, although, with the massive increase of capital investment in public works by the TIPEEG, adherence to the Tender Board Act remained essential to curb large-scale misappropriation of funds through unfair competition and preferential treatment. In mid-December, it was reported that the cabinet had approved another tender exemption for N$ 150 m in emergency spending for the repair of railway lines, allegedly in favour of a company linked to close friends of top officials in the ministry of works and transport. The ministry had previously been accused of being the main culprit when it came to the allocation of large sums for public works without adherence to tender board regulations. On 16 December, the chairperson of the northern branch of the Namibian Chamber of Commerce and Industry (NCCI), in the presence of the finance minister and the director general of the NPC, alleged favouritism and nepotism in awarding tenders under the TIPEEG.

An IPPR report released in December also concluded that mismanagement, lack of transparency and *misappropriation of public funds* were rife in state-owned enterprises, which had mushroomed from 12 to over 60 since independence. Meanwhile, the saga around fraudulent losses of several hundred million Namibian dollars in shady deals through the Development Capital Portfolio of the Government Investment Pension Fund continued. In February, a summary report of the forensic audit was submitted to cabinet and trade union representatives. Details of the massive scale of transactions involving recipients under the banner of Black Economic Empowerment (BEE) were not fully disclosed. In response to public pressure and demands by the trade unions, the cabinet announced on 24 August that it had directed the prosecutor general to lay charges against those officials responsible for the loss and the few politically-well-connected looters who had benefited from the loans.

The finance minister announced at an international *investment* forum at the end of November – during which Ohorongo Cement, a subsidiary of the German company Schwenk, received the international investor award 2011 as the continent's most advanced cement producer – that FDI had increased by 34% during the previous year. This contrasted with the constant net outflow of capital, estimated at between N$ 5 bn and N$ 8 bn. A law reform was initiated to the effect that institutional investors (such as insurance companies, unit trusts and pension funds) should keep a minimum of 35% of their total assets in the country. In early September, the World Economic Forum released its Global Competitiveness Report 2011–12, in which Namibia's ranking dropped from 74th to 83rd out of 142 countries, not least through weak performance in the health and education sectors.

The US-based Wal-Mart Stores Inc. tried to enter the local market through a South African subsidiary. The Namibian Competition Commission and the minister of trade and industry, concerned about the effects of the presence of such a powerful trader on the *retail trade*, tried to prevent this but, on April 28, the retail giant scored a legal victory when the High Court set aside conditions attached to the approval of Wal-Mart's takeover of South Africa's

Massmart group. On 4 November, however, the Supreme Court overturned the ruling and Wal-Mart's objections to the conditions were referred back to the minister.

Mining remained the most important sector in the economy, contributing in 2010 about 15% of GDP and more than 50% of total export revenue. Mines and Energy Minister Isak Katali announced a strategic mineral policy in parliament on 20 April. It transferred control of uranium, copper, gold, zinc and coal to the state-owned Epangelo mining company, including the allocation of exploration and mining licences. The minister admitted that BEE had been exploited in the purchase of exploration licenses, which were secured by local BEE front companies on behalf of foreign-owned companies. Such deals had the sole aim of making "phenomenal amounts" of money for a few to the disadvantage of the state revenue coffers. In July, Katali confirmed rumours that an estimated 12 bn barrels of *oil*, as well as gas, had been identified by exploration companies off the coast. It was announced that systematic drilling would start towards year's end, though a bonanza was not expected to be imminent.

The country remained the world's fourth biggest *uranium* producer. In early December, the wheeling and dealing around the ownership of Swakop Uranium, which controlled the fourth largest known deposit, at Husab, paved the way for further Chinese ownership through a takeover of Kalahari Minerals by China Guangdong Nuclear Power Corp in a £ 632 m ($ 990 m) deal. Kalahari owned 43% in Extract Resources, whose wholly owned subsidiary, Swakop Uranium, received a mining licence to develop Husab as one of the biggest uranium mines in the world. In contrast, the French nuclear fuel and services giant Areva announced on 13 December that it was putting on hold its $ 1 bn investment in the Trekkopje uranium project as a result of worldwide losses of up to $ 2 bn. The originally estimated volume of 45,200 tonnes of uranium was adjusted to 26,000 tonnes, making the investment much less lucrative, since the world market price had dropped from a record high of $ 135 per pound in 2007 to $ 50–$ 55 due to a decline in demand since the Fukushima disaster. Almost bucking this trend, Paladin Energy, owner of the Langer Heinrich uranium mine, announced in late August that new supply agreements had been entered with three US customers with production commitments totalling more than 2.8 m pounds of yellow cake for delivery in 2012–2016. The expansion of Langer Heinrich was expected to increase annual output from 3.7 m pound to 5.2 m pound of yellow cake.

Eastern China Non-Ferrous Metals Investment Holdings, the investment arm of the East China Mineral Exploration and Development Bureau, announced in early December the discovery of 2 bn tonnes of *iron ore* in the Kunene region and plans to open an iron mine and steel plant with an annual production of 5 m tonnes. This promoted speculation about the construction of a third Namibian harbour at Cape Fria, as the government had already allocated funds for a feasibility study in the state budget. NamRights claimed that the Chinese company's local subsidiary had relations with the former head of state, Sam Nujoma, who, according to its investigations, had earlier accepted the role of honorary advisor and senior consultant to the company and received generous donations to his Foundation. Glencore bought 80% of the *zinc* mine at Rosh Pinah, operational since 1969, in a series of transactions during the year. Production during the previous year was reportedly 101,000 tonnes of zinc concentrate and 19,000 tonnes of lead concentrate.

While the Chinese presence in the mining sector expanded further, *trade relations with China* took a dip, according to the NCCI, with a decline in exports from N$ 1.8 bn in 2009 (mainly uranium, copper, lead and other natural resources) to N$ 1.2 bn in 2010. Imports shrank from N$ 2.9 bn in 2009 (mainly cars, telecommunication, furniture, machinery and other manufactured goods) to N$ 1.3 bn in 2010. During a visit to China, Agriculture Minister John Mutorwa signed a bilateral trade agreement on 16 December, which paved the way for the future export of meat and fish, grapes and dates to the Chinese market.

The prolonged negotiations over an *EPA*, which Namibia had refused to sign because of unresolved differences, entered a new chapter with the EU's announcement in October that all preferences in duty- and quota-free market access would end if an EPA were not signed by January 2014. Based on 2009 figures, it was estimated that this would amount to payments of € 58.2 m in duties on Namibian exports to the EU market. Namibia rejected allegations that it was responsible for the delays in finding a solution. On 5 October, Trade Minister Hage Geingob expressed his disappointment and declared that setting such an arbitrary deadline would be no sign of partnership. The continued negotiations towards an adjusted revenue sharing formula among *SACU* member countries, with potentially negative consequences for the public purse in years to come, added to the discouraging indicators with regard to the macroeconomic future and its effects on socioeconomic developments.

Namibia in 2012

The former liberation movement, the South West African People's Organisation (SWAPO), remained in firm political control. Hage Geingob was elected as the party's candidate for the presidential elections scheduled for 2014. In a subsequent cabinet reshuffle and elections to the party's politbureau, 'team Hage' was consolidated. The continued political stability contrasted with modest economic performance and high levels of poverty and unemployment. Foreign policy relations continued to show preferences for friendly links with not so democratic regimes.

Domestic Politics

The 5th *SWAPO Congress*, held from 29 November to 2 December, was preceded by in-fighting over the composition of the 600 delegates, who were to elect the party's leadership. President Pohamba had declared that he remained party president. His unopposed confirmation in office for another five years was a formality. Since his second term as head of state was to end in March 2015, the election of the vice-president implied nomination as the party's *presidential candidate* for the elections in late 2014. Vice-president Hage Geingob (Minister for Trade and Industry) competed for the post with Secretary General and Minister for Justice Pendukeni Iivula-Ithana, and Secretary for Information and Publicity and Minister of Regional and Local Government, Housing and Rural Development, Jerry Ekandjo. Iivula-Ithana was the first woman to be nominated for the post, Geingob the first non-Ovambo-speaker and Ekandjo the first not to have been in exile (and the first to have been a political prisoner on Robben Island). Suspicions that Pohamba was making efforts to impose Geingob, his preferred candidate, on the delegates

© KONINKLIJKE BRILL NV, LEIDEN, 2016 | DOI 10.1163/9789004321571_011

from the 13 regions led to an intense debate as to whether the process was democratic. The eventual result was clearer than expected: in the first round, Geingob received 312 votes, ahead of Ekandjo (220) and Iivula-Ithana (64). Minister for Safety and Security (and Iivula-Ithana's former deputy) Nangolo Mbumba was elected to be the party's *secretary general*. Laura McLeod-Katjirua (governor of the Omaheke region) became his deputy and the only woman to take one of the top four party positions. They had both campaigned for Geingob, who had been the country's first prime minister at independence and was widely considered to be the most suitable statesman. After being demoted by former president Nujoma in 2002, he joined the World Bank's Global Coalition for Africa as executive director in Washington (2003/4), but returned as a SWAPO backbench MP in March 2005.

Elections to the party's 60-member *Central Committee* reproduced old patterns. Women continued to constitute a minority, with 16 members, despite the party's declared policy of gender equality. A *cabinet reshuffle* announced on 4 December re-appointed Geingob as prime minister. Further changes signalled that Pohamba had used his power to anchor the Geingob alliance. 'Team Hage' was further strengthened by the results of elections to the *Politburo* on 11 December, when it snatched several of the 17 seats (four were automatically allocated to the party's top officials). By the end of the year, inner-party changes had set the course for a new chapter in Namibian politics.

The SWAPO Party *Youth League* (SPYL) lost influence. Its candidates for the party's top positions (including Ekandjo) almost all failed. With a reference to the expulsion of the ANC Youth League leader, Julius Malema, Pohamba indicated on 3 March that his generation had steered the liberation struggle and would not accept that over-zealous young Turks did not recognise their merits. Open exchanges by SPYL members on Facebook were criticised as inappropriate forms of critical debate. The SWAPO-affiliated *trade unions* in the National Union of Namibian Workers suffered similar setbacks and were assessed by the end of the year as being at their weakest since independence.

On Cassinga Day (4 May), which commemorates a massacre by the South African army in a refugee camp in Southern Angola, Pohamba categorically rejected the demand by soldiers fighting on the South African side that they be regarded as *war veterans*. This disqualified them from a generous compensation scheme introduced for SWAPO members. High-ranking political office holders and government officials also received a one-off payment and a monthly pension. The rejection of any war veteran status for former combatants on the side of the South African army provoked a debate over the meaning of reconciliation.

Eleven out of 24 *permanent secretaries* were reshuffled as of 1 June, though they merely swopped portfolios. These posts had become political appointments, though the law defined those holding them as top-level civil servants to be appointed purely on professional merit.

On 7 February, the prosecution in the *Caprivi high treason trial* closed its case after its 379th witness testified. The trial had been opened in October 2003, most of the accused having been imprisoned after a failed secession attempt in August 1999. The trial record amounted to almost 35,000 pages. On 28 February, the local EU delegation expressed their hope for a quick end to the legal proceedings. Namibian police banned a demonstration in the Caprivi planned for 12 April to call for the release of the prisoners and a referendum on the status of the Caprivi. On 30 April, the death toll among the imprisoned suspects rose to 19, with 112 men still on trial. More people had already died in custody than were killed during the failed secession attempt. On 10 August, one accused was discharged after the prosecution conceded that there was no evidence on which he could be convicted. The marathon trial had not ended by year's end.

Opposition parties remained ineffective and frustrated over the delay in their court case brought to challenge the results of the November 2009 parliamentary elections. On 21 April, several hundred supporters of eight parties and NGOs marched to the Supreme Court. In another protest, the MPs of the official opposition and other parties left parliament on 25 April amidst booing from SWAPO MPs when Pohamba delivered his State of the Nation Address. On 25 October, the five judges of the Supreme Court dismissed the appeal of the opposition parties against a High Court judgment, which had dismissed their election challenges in February 2011. The election results were thereby confirmed, although the court recognised administrative failures of the Electoral Commission and ruled in favour of the opposition parties' complaint about the conduct of the election.

SWAPO's first policy conference ended on 13 September and declared the *land issue* to be a priority. In an interview with Al Jazeera television on 20 October, Pohamba claimed that the 'willing-buyer, willing-seller' policy had not produced the desired results in land redistribution. He suggested a constitutional change in the rules for the acquisition of land in order to prevent a revolution. According to the commercial farmers' Namibia Agricultural Union, the land reform was on track to meet the targets set for 2020. Of 9,172 registered commercial farms, members of previously disadvantaged groups owned 2,598 and, according to the registered title deeds, 25% of all commercial farmland was in their possession. Meanwhile, illegal fencing off of land in *communal areas* continued. It was confirmed at the 14th annual symposium of the Bank of Namibia on 27 September that the privatisation of collective communal land – dubbed 'modern land grabbing' – implicated holders of political offices at the highest level.

Foreign Affairs

In the 4 December cabinet reshuffle, Foreign Minister Utoni Nujoma (who was transferred to his previous portfolio as minister of justice) was replaced by Minister for Environment and Tourism Netumbo

Nandi-Ndaitwah. She had been the deputy foreign minister at independence and was a member of 'team Hage'.

South Africa's President Jacob Zuma visited on 29 February to 1 March. Consultations included the situation in Zimbabwe. Namibia's government remained a strong ally of Mugabe, and Zuma reportedly sought to influence the government's role in support of a compromise solution. President Pohamba spoke at a high-level UN debate on the rule of law on 24 September and the opening of the General Assembly the next day. He carried out his first official state visit to South Africa on 5–7 November. Throughout the year he was vocal in calling for the UNSC to be reformed to give Africa a permanent seat.

Friendly ties with other *African countries* were underlined by several state visits. Pohamba visited Maputo on 29 March, where fishing quotas were allocated to companies of both countries with respect to each other's waters. State visits were paid by President Ian Khama of Botswana on 25–27 June and by King Mswati III of Swaziland, accompanied by one of his 12 wives, on 24–28 July. The latter visit included a hunting safari with former president Sam Nujoma and some sightseeing excursions. With much less fanfare, Togolese President Faure Gnassingbe paid a state visit on 9–11 October.

Namibia's friendship with *Cuba* was recognised in a donation of wild animals to the latter's national zoo. A first freight plane left for Havana in mid-November. While the government remained tight-lipped over the operation, the cost of the gift was estimated at around $ 30 m.

Bilateral relations with *Germany* remained strained over the colonial legacy. The 100th anniversary celebrations of the equestrian monument erected in memory of German soldiers killed fighting the local population took place at end of January in the presence of apologetic colonial delegates from Germany. The minister of information, speaking for the government, criticised this as insensitive provocation. It coincided with the official visit of Walter Lindner,

Director General of African Affairs in the German Foreign Office, on 1–3 February for high-level meetings. He confirmed the reactivation of a special initiative, which earmarked € 20 m for projects to the benefit of historically affected communities. Since independence, Germany had allocated some € 700 m in bilateral aid. Lindner visited Namibia again on 14–15 May, without matters being resolved. The German ambassador to Namibia, Egon Kochanke, replaced Lindner in Berlin from August.

Relations with the *EU* improved through an addendum to the 10th European Development Fund country strategy signed on 12 March. It added € 26.6 m (N$ 260 m) to top up the granted € 131.5 m in recognition of the well administered funds to achieve three of the MDGs concerning water and sanitation, maternal and child mortality. At a EU-Namibia Political Dialogue held on 7 March with a special focus on the *EPA* the EU's local head of delegation stressed the role of the union and its member states as by far biggest donors. Namibia's foreign minister at the same occasion warned against restrictions planned for the export of beef, dessert grapes and fish to the EU market if the EPA was not signed. Europe receives 30% of Namibia's exports and is its largest market outside the region. At the 7th Summit of Heads of State and Government of ACP countries in Malabo, Equatorial Guinea, in mid-December, newly appointed Prime Minister Hage Geingob and his successor at the trade ministry, Calle Schlettwein, reiterated their determination not to sign an EPA that limited development to trade without adding value to raw materials before export.

The deputy minister for trade and industry declared at a business forum with a Chinese delegation on 6 March that *China* was an alternative market. Chinese Foreign Minister Yang Jiechi visited Namibia on 5–6 January. He signed another technical cooperation agreement for N$ 26 m (20 m yuan). Jiechi described Namibia as an "all-weather friend", but advised the adoption of an omni-directional policy – or relations with the East, the West, and any other regional configuration – while reiterating that China was there to stay. On 26 March, Theo Ben Gurirab, former foreign minister and prime minister, now speaker of the national assembly, addressed a delegation of Chinese MPs headed by the vice chairperson of the standing committee of the National People's Congress, Hua Jiamin. He strongly criticised Western military and economic hegemony and warned that "military intervention and regime change have replaced dialogue and peaceful co-existence". During a three-day visit, Chinese Deputy Prime Minister Hui Lianghui signed another five cooperation agreements on 2 April.

On 15 March, the Kavango-Zambezi *Transfrontier Conservation Area* was launched at Katima Mulilo in the Caprivi. The world's largest trans-frontier conservation area is situated within the Kavango and Zambezi River basins and spans over 444,000 km².

Socioeconomic Developments

With beginning of the year, Fitch Ratings downgraded the *credit rating* outlook from "positive" to "stable", as a result of the greater-than-expected impact of the government's increased spending plan on Namibia's public debt, set to double to 33% of GDP by 2013/14.

In early April, it was disclosed that the latest *corruption* perception report by the Anti-Corruption Commission (ACC) showed that more than half of all Namibians interviewed in all 13 regions of the country considered the level of corruption as very high. The ACC also confirmed on 4 April that it had investigated bribery allegations in connection with the big Neckartal dam tender. The bidding process for the project, valued at more than N$ 2 bn, was put on hold due to assumed malpractices. A survey by the local Institute for Public Policy Research warned In June of a high level of government corruption at local and regional levels, which was not being adequately dealt with by law enforcement initiatives and the ACC. A report released on 17 December by Global Financial Integrity on *illicit financial flows* from developing countries between 2001 and

2010 estimated there to be an average annual transfer of around $ 420 m (about N$ 3.6 bn) in 'dirty money'.

On 28 February, Finance Minister Saara Kuugongelwa-Amadhila presented the *annual budget for 2012/13*. It emphasised fiscal discipline, despite another increase of N$ 2.5 bn (8%). The estimate of revenues of N$ 35.4 bn (34.6% of GDP) – an increase of 32% – was based on an anticipated previously unpredicted surge in revenue from the SACU pool from N$ 7.1 bn to N$ 13.9 bn. Total estimated expenditure increased from N$ 37.7 bn for 2011/12 to N$ 40.2 bn (39.2% of GDP), with a budget deficit of 4.6% of GDP. The total debt was calculated at N$ 28.3 bn or 27.7% of GDP. The operational budget accounted for 77% of expenditure and the development budget for 17%, with 6% spent on statutory payments (i.e. servicing debt). The highest allocations were again for education (N$ 9.4 bn or 23.4%), followed by health and social services with close to N$ 4 bn (9.9%). Observers criticised the modest increase of state pensions by N$ 50 to N$ 550. Taxes on alcohol and tobacco were raised by between 5% and 20%. Opposition parties bemoaned the continued bail out of parastatals, such as the national airline and the national radio and television broadcaster, which produced notorious deficits. Another matter of concern was the budgetary increase for the security apparatus (military, police, intelligence). The budget also revealed estimated increases for subsistence and travel allowances for civil servants from 2010/11 to 2014/15 by 54% to N$ 1.7 bn.

The *IMF* country report released in mid-February urged the government to create sound fiscal buffers and to reign in its spending as a protective measure against global economic shocks. It expressed concern about the plunging of international reserves, standing at $ 1.4 bn at the end of 2011 compared with $ 1.9 bn at the end of 2009. The 2012 Article IV Consultation Mission visited Windhoek from 29 October to 9 November. It adjusted its prognosis to 4% economic growth for the year and recommended policies to counteract the negative impact of inequality by targeted investment in health and education. Figures released by the Bank of Namibia on

13 December for the third quarter of the year indicated poor performances in all economic sectors except mining, construction, transport and communications. The targeted annual *economic growth
rate* of 4.6% became unrealistic. A best-case scenario suggested
anything between 3% and 3.5%.

The *fishing industry* continued to struggle. Minister of Fisheries
and Marine Resources Bernhard Esau complained at the end of
February about the "bail out" attitude by fishing companies, who
assumed that the government needed to secure employment by
compensating for the limited allowed catches and increased costs
and setting higher fishing quotas. He maintained that this attitude
defeated the purpose of proper fish management and put sustainable development at risk. *Tourism* suffered from the global financial
crisis with an 11.2% decline in European visitors in 2011 compared
with 2010. Over 75% of the more than a million foreign arrivals came
from other African countries (a third of all foreign visitors were
from Angola). *Agriculture* showed mixed results. The export of seed-
less dessert grapes mainly to the UK and the Far and Middle East
markets was expected to decline from a record of 4.7 m cartons (of
4.5 kg each) in 2011 to 3.5 m as a result of a cold winter. In contrast,
cereal production increased by 42% from 117,000 tonnes in 2011 to
166,000 tonnes. Uncertainty caused by the volatility of the exchange
rate, the Euro crisis and a slow-down in demand from India and
China, as well as a general liquidity shortage on financial markets,
affected the *diamond industry*. Total sales by local cutting and polishing companies stood at about N$ 1.5 bn (from N$ 1.6 bn in 2011).
Namdeb Holdings produced about 1.6 m carats, of which some 40%
were processed locally.

Mining operations remained the economic backbone, despite
the French multinational Areva's decision to postpone the launch
of the Trekkopje uranium mine due to a decline in world market prices. Trekkopje was expected to become the largest uranium mine in Southern Africa. Operations by a joint venture with
Chinese partners started construction of the N$ 12 bn uranium

mine at Husab near Swakopmund towards the end of the year. Husab is the third largest known uranium deposit in the world, with a production potential of 15 m pounds of uranium oxide per year. Once operational, the country would rank as the world's second largest producer. Chinese investments were also announced for the Omitiomire copper mine deposit 120 km north-east of Windhoek.

Plans to develop the *Gecko industrial park* with a phosphate mine, a harbour, sulfuric and phosphoric acid, soda ash and bicarbonate plants, a coal-fired power station, a desalination plant and further heavy industry, in the Dorob National Park near Swakopmund, stirred vehement local protest. Plans to invest N$ 13 bn in a chemo-industrial complex in a highly sensitive environment provoked concerns about potential damage, and fear of negative impacts on tourism and fishing.

The public energy utility NamPower announced on 30 March a critical supply period for *electricity* due to power supply problems from South Africa's Eskom and the end of a power purchase agreement with the Zimbabwean power utility Zesa in 2013. A supply deficit of 80 MW was anticipated for the forthcoming winter period, expected to grow to 150 MW by the end of 2013 and to 300 MW by 2015. It was announced in August that a coal-fired power station at an investment cost of between N$ 4–7 bn would be fast-tracked, while the potential exploration of the Kudu gas power project off the coast at an estimated cost of N$ 9 bn was shelved.

In July, discoveries of large *water reserves* in the northern part of Namibia made headlines. According to a geo-hydrological survey of the Etosha-Cuvelai basin, an estimated 5 bn m³ of groundwater existed at a depth of some 280–350 m. It was projected to be able to supply fresh water to the region (which is home to some 40% of the country's population) for an estimated 400 years.

Preliminary *demographic results* of the 2011 National Housing and Population Census released on 11 April by the National Planning Commission indicated an annual average population growth since 2001 of 1.5% from 1.8 m to 2.1 m people. This was considered manageable in relation to an annual average economic growth of 4.7% during the same period. Fifty-one per cent of Namibians were female, and 58% lived in rural areas. The reliability of the data was another matter: the most densely populated area, which includes the capital, Windhoek, was the Khomas region, with 340,900 people, but estimates provided earlier by the city's municipal council had suggested that the number of residents in the capital alone exceeded 400,000.

On World Malaria Day (25 April), the health minister reported that *malaria* cases and related deaths had fallen between 2001 (624,384 reported cases with 1,681 deaths) and 2011 (15,905 cases with 10 deaths reported) by 97% and 98% respectively. Data on *HIV/ AIDS also* indicated a decline. According to an update released by the Ministry of Health on 13 December, the infection rate had fallen from 18.8% in 2010 to 18.2%. The most positive trend was among the 15–24 age group, where it had fallen from 14.2% in 2006 to 8.9%. The global report released by UNAIDS in November indicated that the number of new local infections had fallen by more than 50% since 2001. Some 107,000 people received antiretroviral therapy. However, the Global Fund, as main funder of HIV/AIDS, tuberculosis and malaria programmes, announced as a result of an audit report released on 2 October that about N$ 14.85 m of released funds should be recovered due to unaccounted or unapproved spending. The Fund had granted in total $ 200 m (N$ 1.8 bn) by 2011, of which N$ 1.3 bn had been disbursed.

Unemployment, announced to be 51.2% in 2011 and contested since then, was scrutinised by a team from the World Bank at the request of the Namibian authorities. Their findings, presented on 20 February, did not deviate significantly from the official survey results, with a broad unemployment rate estimated at 45.5%–48.8% and 30.5%–34.1% on a stricter definition of unemployment. In contrast, an independent local report presented in early June stressed that the figures remained too high. Surprisingly, the finance minister declared at the SPYL congress during the first weekend of September that the Targeted Intervention Programme for Employment and Economic Growth, announced in 2011 with much fanfare, would serve to stimulate business first and job creation only as a secondary consideration.

The Labour Amendment Act of 2012 was gazetted on 12 April. Its regulations limited the controversial *labour hire regulations*. In his May Day speech, Pohamba urged the Ministry of Labour to implement the law effectively in order to protect casual workers, estimated by the employers' federation to number 16,000. Labour hire companies complained that job losses were inevitable. It was reported in August that an estimated 80% of those in temporary employment through labour hire companies no longer had work or income.

In early February, the permanent secretary of the Ministry of Labour and Social Welfare disclosed figures from 2008, according to which almost half the population were living in *poverty*. Data from the Central Bureau of Statistics maintained that 27.4% of the country's population were classified as poor, with monthly income below N$ 265, while 22.6% were considered as severely poor, with monthly income below N$ 184. Data released by the Namibia Statistics Agency in November suggested a decline in the overall gap between rich and poor between 1993 and 2010, while deep pockets of absolute poverty remained, with the rural population, women and the elderly as the most vulnerable. Kavango was the poorest region, while Erongo was best off. The Caprivi and Khomas regions recorded an increase in poverty. The Gini-coefficient (measuring income discrepancies) remained among the highest in the world at about 0.6. A FAO report on the state of food insecurity in the world, released on 9 October, disclosed that almost 34% of all Namibians were chronically hungry – significantly more than the global average of 12.5% and higher than the average in Africa (22.9%) and Sub-Saharan Africa (26.8%). Undernourishment had increased since the turn of the century (then at 24.9%). In contrast, Health Minister

Richard Kamwi confirmed in parliament on 23 October that almost half of the MPs were either overweight or obese.

During November, teachers and other civil servants went on strike for salary increases. A rise of 8% was finally conceded after tough negotiations and prolonged absences from work. *Public service salary increases* amounted to some N$ 320 m and left a financial gap in the annual budget. The Public Office Bearers' Remuneration and Benefits Commission made its report public on 18 December. It urged the president to increase salaries for the highest-ranking public/political office holders by an average of over 30% and in some cases up to 80%, which caused public uproar.

The National Agenda for Children 2012–2016 was launched in mid-June. Prime Minister Nahas Angula revealed that almost a third of *children* under five were stunted or small for their age because of malnutrition. On 7 August, the Ministry of Health and Social Services disclosed that 10% of newborns were fed plain water during the first two months, only one third of the population had access to improved sanitation facilities and almost a quarter of deaths of children under five were related to diarrhoea-type diseases. With an estimated 1.3 m people without proper toilet facilities, Namibia had one of the lowest levels of sanitation coverage in the sub-region. On 13 August, Pohamba constituted the first-ever presidential commission of enquiry to investigate the state of public health services resulting response to the increase in the number of deaths of babies, mothers and other patients in hospitals.

The UN Special Rapporteur on the rights of indigenous peoples, James Anaya, assessed the living conditions of *minority groups* during a one-week visit in September. He diagnosed a lack of coherent government policies that assigned positive values to the identities and practices of indigenous people. In early October, the UN Special Rapporteur on extreme *poverty and human rights*, Magdalena Sepúlveda, visited for an eight-day fact-finding mission. Her preliminary report concluded that progress in poverty reduction had been slow.

Namibia in 2013

2013 was a transitional year between the appointment of the future political leadership of the governing South West African People's Organisation (SWAPO) at the end of 2012 and the parliamentary and presidential elections at the end of 2014. The general macroeconomic performance remained stable while aggrandizement of the new elite and the lack of public services and delivery for many continued. A serious drought added to the misery.

Domestic Politics

During the year, the top brass of SWAPO, newly elected to take over political leadership in government after the parliamentary and presidential elections due to take place towards the end of 2014, became further strengthened. *Team Hage* (named after Prime Minister Hage Geingob, who was the party's presidential candidate) was able to expand its control over strategic positions in the party governance structure. President Pohamba also appointed several supporters of Geingob to higher-ranking positions in the public administration. The list of ten deputies appointed to the party secretariat at the end of May included only supporters of Team Hage. The party's founding president, Sam Nujoma, addressing a party rally in the first weekend of June, endorsed for the first time the result of the election held at the party congress in November 2012 and thereby signalled acceptance of Team Hage. The fact that this was considered an important message underlined the elder statesman's continuing relevance for daily politics.

This ended speculation concerning 'the old man's' preferences and corrected the impression created by the *SWAPO Youth League*, who supported another candidate. In a statement on 29 May, the Youth League suggested that Nujoma agreed with them, and made

© KONINKLIJKE BRILL NV, LEIDEN, 2016 | DOI 10.1163/9789004321571_012

a scathing attack on Geingob. The Youth League leaders were taken to task for this attack at the party's central committee meeting on 14 June. Several high-ranking party officials called for the leadership to be axed for misbehaviour at the forthcoming extra-ordinary congress, but Pohamba intervened by asking for an apology instead of taking disciplinary action. The apology was officially tendered and confirmed the political defeat of the Youth League, which had for some time been trying to gain more influence in the party.

Delegates at the extra-ordinary congress held on 22–24 June in Swakopmund amended the party constitution by stipulating, among other things, 50/50 representation of men and women in all party organs and structures. This *gender parity* was enthusiastically welcomed by female delegates but met with concern among men, and debates began as to how sure the predominantly male leadership would be of retaining their positions in office after the next elections.

On 18 January, Pohamba appointed the fourth *Delimitation Commission*, tasked with (re-)determining regional and constituency boundaries. Based on its recommendations, Pohamba announced on 8 August the creation of 14 new constituencies in nine regions. The Kavango region was split into Kavango East and Kavango West, increasing the number of regions to 14. The Karas Region was spelt in the vernacular as !Karas (later adjusted to //Karas), and the Caprivi Region was renamed Zambezi, giving rise to protests from some local inhabitants who considered the name change as a denial of their regional identity. Part of the region's population had previously sought greater autonomy from the rest of the Namibian state and territory, which had culminated in a failed violent secessionist uprising in August 1999, and the subsequent treason trial was still ongoing during 2013. Objections were also raised by some of the residents in Lüderitzbucht to the announced change in the name of both the constituency and the town to Naminüs. The change in the name of the town remained pending after it was established that this decision did not lie within the discretion of the president but rested with the town council as the local authority. On 3 September, a coalition of civil society agencies called for the release of the Delimitation Commission's report, which was not made public.

An *electoral law reform* process was initiated, with a Law Reform and Development Commission tasked to review electoral procedures. In early November, the commission reported back to the prime minister and the Electoral Commission of Namibia. The briefing was also attended by invited civil society organisations. The commission announced the tabling of four bills in parliament. Given the long-lasting legal contestations after the last parliamentary elections, preparations for the next elections were closely followed and remained a contentious issue.

In a speech on 27 November, Sam Nujoma gave a first taste of things to come in the forthcoming *election year*. He blamed civil servants for non-delivery, calling this an act of sabotage of government programmes and dubbing them "elements of Koevoet", a special army unit established by the South Africans to fight SWAPO but dissolved at Independence. At the party's politburo meeting in early December, Nujoma (using his entitlement to attend all party meetings as an honorary member), reportedly called for a national referendum to address the *land issue* but was informed that this would be unconstitutional.

The removal of the colonial *equestrian monument* in a surprise action on 25 December led to speculation that this was a prelude to government initiatives to establish its strength and appeal to anti-colonial sentiments. The statue was a prominent marker in Windhoek's memory landscape and a popular tourist attraction. Parts of the local German speaking community reacted with shock and dismay to its removal, which came as a surprise despite earlier discussions over the future of the highly symbolic monument, and led to widespread discussion and controversy.

The government continued to adopt a lenient stance on abuses of office by high-ranking civil servants and politicians involved in private businesses, which were tantamount to *embezzlement and corruption.* Large-scale transactions in the property market, mainly in Windhoek, as well as dubious practices in the awarding of tenders for public works, were indicative of a network of business interests benefitting from privileged information and preferential treatment. On 10 December, the Institute of Public Policy Research released a critical report on the lack of relevant anti-corruption legislation in non-compliance with the United Nations Convention Against Corruption, which had been signed by Namibia in 2003. TI's Corruption Perception Index released at the end of November ranked Namibia 57th (up one place from 58th in 2012) out of 177 countries. On 12 November, the auditor general disclosed that 11 ministries had failed during the past financial year to account for a total of N$ 15 m spent on travel and subsistence allowances.

The Reporters Without Borders Index on the state of *media freedom* released in November ranked Namibia 19th out of 179 countries, two places higher than in the 2011–12 index, and ahead of several Western democracies (Belgium, Canada and the USA). On 2 May, the UN Special Rapporteur on the Rights of the Indigenous People, James Anaya, published his report based on a fact-finding mission during September the year before. He maintained that, despite significant achievements in overcoming the destructive legacies of colonialism and apartheid, *indigenous groups*, particularly the San and the Himba, remained marginalised.

Foreign Affairs

Namibia's foreign policy had a relatively low profile during the year. It maintained an emphasis on good relations in the sub-region and the continent. On 6–7 November, President Jacob Zuma of *South Africa* made an official state visit, when he and President Pohamba stressed the need for even closer cooperation and underlined the importance of the bi-lateral commission established the year before. Sub-divided into four sectoral committees, the commission had as one of its key functions the practical implementation of the 52 agreements and memoranda of understanding already entered into. A state visit by President Goodluck Jonathan of *Nigeria* announced for 9–10 May was cancelled one day ahead of his expected arrival; no official reason was given, but the cancellation was probably related to reported internal unrest in Nigeria.

Iran reactivated and intensified earlier relations with Namibia by re-opening an embassy after 15 years. Iranian Foreign Minister Ali Akbar Salehi visited Windhoek on 8–9 July for the opening ceremony and stressed Iran's interest in closer collaboration with Namibia as the continent's fourth largest exporter of non-fuel minerals. Namibia's Navy Commander Admiral Peter Villo headed a delegation of the Namibian Defence Force visiting Tehran on 10 October. He announced that the two countries planned to cooperate more closely on naval training and experience in manufacturing maritime facilities, given the common maritime threats.

Pohamba was appointed chairperson of the SADC *Organ for Security* at the SADC Summit on 18 August. On 10 September, the first Troika meeting to be held in Windhoek discussed the security situation in eastern DRC, and the political situation in Madagascar and Zimbabwe.

Speaking at the 68th UN General Assembly on 26 September, Pohamba focused on the MDGs. He used the opportunity to reiterate that the elections in *Zimbabwe* had been free, fair and credible and urged that Western countries should lift sanctions. Pohamba and Zuma had congratulated ZANU-PF and Robert Mugabe on their re-election at a time when no reports from election observers had yet been released.

Pohamba made a state visit to *Finland* on 13–14 November. Finland remained a donor country. During the year, its embassy in Windhoek was upgraded by the appointment of a new ambassador, the only one from a Nordic country. Pohamba then attended the *Commonwealth Heads of State summit* in Malaysia and made the first state visit to *Vietnam* by a Namibian president.

EU Commissioner for Trade Karel de Gucht visited on 16 June for further exchanges over the *EPA* with the prime minister and the minister for trade and industry. Despite increased pressure on Namibia to sign the Interim EPA, the government remained steadfast and refused to give in, since, in its view, the agreement would damage the country's economic interests by, among other things, preventing the implementation of an infant industry protection policy as a step towards industrialisation.

The 11th Conference of the Parties (COP11) to the *UN Convention to Combat Desertification* (UNCCD), which was attended by over 3,000 international delegates, took place over two weeks in Windhoek and ended on 28 September. Minister of Environment and Tourism Uahekua Herunga, who was the COP11 president, said the conference had strengthened the UNCCD as an agent of sustainable development. He presented the "Namib Declaration on a stronger United Nations Convention to Combat Desertification for a land degradation neutral world", which called on stakeholders to commit themselves to enhanced sustainable land management and improved livelihoods at all levels.

Socioeconomic Developments

The latest *demographic statistics*, compiled during August 2011 by the Population and Housing Census, were released at the end of March. The total population was given as 2,113,077, showing an annual growth rate of 1.4% since 2001. Almost 52% were female, 56.5% were aged between 15 and 59 years, 23% between five and 14 years, 13% were younger than five years and 7% were 60 or older. 57% lived in rural areas (down from 67% in 2001); urbanisation had increased by 15% since 1991. More than half of the population lived either in traditional dwellings (38%) or in shacks (16%). The main language for almost half the population (49%) was Oshiwambo, followed by Nama/Damara (11.3%) and Afrikaans (10.4%), with only 3.4% of households having the official language English as a main language. The *labour force* was given as 847,415, with 312,503 (36.9%) unemployed. The Namibia Labour Force Survey 2012 was released in April and gave the number of unemployed as 238,174 or 27.4% out of an active work force of 868,268. Those registered as jobless were 56% of youths aged between 15 and 19, 49% of those in the age group 20–24, and only 13% of 50–54-year-olds. Most importantly, the figures confirmed the growing relevance of the younger segment in the population, which emerged as an increasingly strategic policy factor to reckon with since Independence.

On 5 March, Finance Minister Saara Kuugongelwa-Amadhila presented the *annual budget* for the 2013–14 financial year. Overall expenditure was expected to rise by 19% to N$ 47.6 bn (from N$ 39.9 bn in 2012), with a growth in current expenditure of 23% and capital expenditure estimated to increase by only 11%. This was a proportional decline from 6.3% to 6.1% of the total budget, representing a reduction of investment in and maintenance of infrastructure. The highest budget allocations were, as in previous years, to education (N$ 10.8 bn), followed by health and social services (N$ 5.3 bn), but defence (N$ 3.96 bn) and safety and security (N$ 3.8 bn) added up jointly to the second highest allocation. A major cost factor remained the bloated civil service, with an increase in personnel costs of over 230% since 2003–4 to N$ 17.5 bn, more than 40% of the total budget. Statutory expenditure, i.e. interest payments on public debts and loan guarantees for mainly state-owned enterprises rose to 4.7% of total expenditure. Revenue income was expected to increase by 8.2% to N$ 40.1 bn, leaving an anticipated deficit of N$ 7.5 bn or 6.4% of GDP. Additional borrowing increased debts to N$ 32.4 bn or 27.8% of GDP. The main source of anticipated income was once again from the SACU revenue pool and was expected to be N$ 14.7 bn or 37% of total revenue for the financial year, while taxes on income and profits of individuals and companies was estimated at 35% and value added tax at 21%. The tax threshold for individual income was raised from N$ 40,000 to N$ 50,000 a year with an entry level set at 18% (down from 27%). All tax brackets were lowered except for the highest income segment, which remained at 37% on income above N$ 1.5 m a year. Corporation tax was reduced from 34% to 33%.

It was estimated that the combined tax relief increased *domestic spending* power by N$ 1.2 bn. According to the Namibian Consumer Price Index released on 12 November by the Namibian Statistics Agency, consumption patterns had changed considerably between 1993–94 and 2009–10: expenditure on alcoholic beverages had almost quadrupled, while spending on education and food had fallen substantially. Expenditure on communications (in particular mobile phones and internet) had increased dramatically, and spending on public utilities (water, electricity) as well as gas and fuel also absorbed a higher proportion of expenditure.

The annual *inflation* rate for 2012 was at 6.5%, according to a Bank of Namibia announcement in February. A prognosis released in August estimated that the rate for 2013 would be slightly above 6%. The economic growth rate for 2012 was 5%, with a forecast by the Bank of Namibia of 4.7% for 2013, while the IMF expected 4.2%. The GDP for 2012 was over US$ 12 bn. Given that the local Namibian Dollar (N$) was an internationally non-convertible currency and pegged to the South African Rand, the deteriorating *currency exchange rate* had massively contributed to rises in import prices. As from mid-year, the purchase price of the Euro had increased from 13 to 15 Rand and of the US$ from 9 to 11 Rand. While this suited export-oriented production, it had a negative effect on the rate of inflation by causing price increases, mainly for luxury consumer goods.

Mining activities benefitted from attractive world market prices for base metals and other minerals. North River Resources announced plans to re-open the lead and zinc mine near several uranium sites that had been closed in 1992, as the prices justified new production. Dundee Precious Metals confirmed that the sulphuric acid plant being built in Tsumeb with an investment of some N$ 3 bn was on track. Among the biggest capital projects in Namibian history, the new plant was expected to be operational towards the end of 2014. It was intended that the sulphuric acid generated would solve an environmental problem caused by the release of sulphur dioxide during the blister copper manufacturing process at the Tsumeb smelter; 90% of the expected production would be sold to Rössing Uranium. The multinational Anglo American announced for de Beers, the holding company for Namdeb, a 6% increase in its annual *diamond* production from 1,667,000 carats in 2012 to 1,762,000 carats in 2013.

Uranium production continued to be among the important income and employment generating activities, despite lower world market prices in the aftermath of Fukushima, in view of which initiatives towards improved institutionalisation and regulation took place. During March, a draft Nuclear Cycle Policy was finalised in cooperation with the Finnish Radiation and Nuclear Safety Authority, which was designed as a guiding document for exploration, mining, enrichment and nuclear power. It was expected to be finalised in 2014. The Namibian Uranium Association was established on 18 November as a kind of watchdog representing Namibian interests in the industry. It brought together stakeholders, experiencing common woes as a result of the low world market prices for uranium oxide, which rendered several big operations unprofitable. It emerged that, Rössing and Langer Heinrich, two of the biggest operations, had reduced production. The French Areva, which was developing its Trekkopje mine, and other investors had put large investments on hold. In contrast, construction at the Husab mine being developed by Swakop Uranium with Chinese investment to become the world's second largest mine, with full production after completion estimated at 6,800 tonnes a year, continued according to plan, but with complaints about the shortage of qualified workers and no secure long-term solution for water and energy supplies. Between 2007 and 2012 more than 30 companies from Australia,

Canada, China and Russia had been engaged in uranium exploration activities, despite a moratorium on new prospecting licences.
During the same period, annual uranium production had increased
by almost 50% to about 4,500 tonnes a year. Other future mining
sites included Valencia (developed by the Canadian Forsys Metals)
and Etango (by the Australian Bannerman Resources). The OECD
estimated future uranium production from new mining activities at
11,000 to 13,000 tonnes per annum, which would equal one-fifth to
one-quarter of the current global supply from mining.

Namibia slipped 11 places in the *Ease of Doing Business* ranking
from 87th to 98th out of 189 countries. Similarly, Namibia's ranking
in the *Economic Freedom Report* 2013, based on 2011 data and compiled by the Fraser 80 Institute, deteriorated from 88th to 97th out
of 152 countries. The ranking is based on five components. Namibia
did well in two of them, namely Legal System and Property Rights
(ranked 27th) and Regulation (50th), while falling behind in Size
of Government (99th), Sound Money (referring to money supply
and inflation, ranked 113th) and Freedom to Trade Internationally
(117th). In the *Global Competitiveness Report* issued in September by
the World Economic Forum for 2013–14, Namibia was among the top
five performers in Africa and improved its ranking by two places to
90th of 148 countries.

Data presented in the UNDP's *Human Development Report* in
2013 disclosed socioeconomic disparities. An annual average Gross
National Income per capita of almost US$ 6,000 classified Namibia
as a higher middle-income country. It ranked 101st out of 186 countries. The HDI, however, was at 0.608, which placed Namibia at 128th,
i.e. 27 places lower. The discrepancy increased further with the Gini-
coefficient. On a scale between 0 (absolute distributive equality
among all persons) and 1 (where everything is allocated to one person only), Namibia, with .639, had the highest Gini-coefficient of all
countries measured. The Inequality-adjusted HDI, which combined
social inequality with the HDI ranking, was another 16 places lower,
the third highest downward adjustment of all countries.

According to UNICEF figures released on World Toilet Day (19 November), 52% of the country's population had no access to proper *sanitation facilities*. This placed Namibia among the countries with the highest proportion of people in the world who had to defecate in the open, considered as one of the main causes of diarrhoea, which was the third most common cause of hospital attendance and the second highest cause of pediatric admissions in the country. A report issued on 18 November by the African Child Policy Forum, based on indicators from all available child-related indexes, ranked Namibia as 26th out of 52 African countries in terms of child-friendliness, defined as making the maximum effort to meet its obligations to respect, protect and fulfil the rights and *wellbeing of children*. This was a downgrade by 24 places compared with the 2008 index, the biggest decline among all countries on the continent. The main reasons given for the dramatic deterioration were reductions in government spending on sectors benefitting children, a fall in levels of performance concerning translation of resources into child wellbeing, and a poor record for access to international legal instruments and the domestication of child rights.

More positive were efforts to combat HIV/AIDS. Figures announced during World AIDS Day at the beginning of December showed that the HIV infection rate had fallen between 2001 and 2011 by 68% and AIDS-related deaths by 44%; 83% of HIV-positive mothers received antiretroviral treatment and mother-to-child transmission was reduced dramatically. However, there remained a surge in new infections in the 10–19 age group. On a visit in early December, UNDP Administrator Helen Clark attested that Namibia was making "good progress" in achieving the *MDGs*, though many of the defined targets remained unmet. UNICEF regional director Steven Allen, who visited at the same time, identified shortcomings in access to primary and secondary schooling, a dire need of qualified teachers and a lack of quality education.

A bad rainy season during the first months of the year led to the worst *drought* for 30 years. According to a report submitted to

Cabinet in May, an estimated 330,900 people were directly affected by hunger and food insecurity, with a further 400,000 people estimated to be in medium-term need of food assistance. In response to reports that several people had died of starvation, Prime Minister Geingob stated in parliament in mid-October that malnourishment and hunger existed not only because of drought but as a daily feature of life for less well-off people.

Namibia in 2014

The second half of the year was dominated by preparations and campaigning for the national and presidential elections at the end of November. The dominant South West African People's Organisation (SWAPO), the former liberation movement, in political power since Independence, retained its political hegemony as expected and even extended its control in the legislature. The SWAPO parliamentary majority adopted far-reaching constitutional amendments in August, including increasing the number of seats in the National Assembly and the National Council as from the next five-year term, and adding to the executive powers of Hage Geingob as the next elected head of state. Foreign policy continued with a 'looking East' orientation, while the controversial EPA was finally signed. Macroeconomic data suggested little change in terms of both socioeconomic trends and the stark inequalities in the distribution of wealth. Social protest against government policy was on the increase, with mounting confrontations, though the general climate remained one of relative stability.

Domestic Politics

The *growing frustration* over government expenditure on infrastructure, which was considered unnecessary and as only serving the symbolic architecture of those in political power, erupted on 13 January with a protest march by around 100 mainly young people in Windhoek. They demonstrated against allocation by the cabinet, reported in local print media, of N$ 700 m for the construction of a new parliament building. The 'Tintenpalast' (ink palace), the administrative building complex dating back to German colonial rule and home of the National Assembly, was considered an anachronistic relic that should be replaced. The youth demonstrators, not

© KONINKLIJKE BRILL NV, LEIDEN, 2016 | DOI 10.1163/9789004321571_013

visibly affiliated to any political party, handed over a petition, which demanded that the money should be spent on more important priorities in the light of massive youth unemployment and a deteriorating health sector. On 19 February, physical violence erupted in a squatter camp on the outskirts of Windhoek's former township, Katutura, when police demolished one of the illegal shacks erected there; stone throwers damaged several police vehicles.

Social protest also mounted through a group organised in the Namibian Exile Kids Association (NEKA) and escalated into the *killing of a demonstrator*. NEKA had been formed by young Namibians born in exile, who (often as orphans) came to independent Namibia without patronage or family connections to the new political elite. They had complained for years about the lack of integration and employment opportunities and had articulated their growing frustration in various forms of peaceful protest. On 27 August, NEKA activists once again demonstrated outside SWAPO headquarters. Police dispersed the crowd with tear gas and opened fire. A fleeing young mother was shot in the back and died on the spot.

Activists of the *SWAPO Party Youth League* (SPYL) condemned this repressive act and the SPYL leadership, in open defiance of party solidarity, attended the funeral of the victim in her northern Namibia home village instead of the launch of the party manifesto in Windhoek. From within the ranks of SPYL officials also emerged the most spectacular forms of protest seen thus far. Its Secretary of Information Job Amupanda together with two other leading activists symbolically occupied an urban plot in an up-market Windhoek suburb on 9 November. Later dubbed an *'affirmative repositioning'*, this initiative expressed frustration over speculative land deals in Windhoek by members of the political municipal administration. Such property transactions were profitable only to a few selected cronies, while ordinary citizens could not afford to purchase plots. The SWAPO leadership (president, secretary general and their deputies) immediately suspended the SPYL activists. After being informed that the authority to suspend them rested solely with the members of the party's much larger Politbureau, they declared that this was a matter of urgency that required immediate intervention. Despite such new dissent, the elections shortly afterwards remained peaceful and without any spectacular events or surprises.

On 27 August, the National Assembly adopted a new *Electoral Bill*, which introduced, among other things, the use of electronic voting machines. The law stipulated that a paper trail was required to visibly confirm to the voter the choice made. But then the Indian company that had delivered the equipment announced that it was impossible to comply with the law without testing the technology. The elections held end of November therefore violated the legal provision that had been adopted.

The SWAPO parliamentary majority also voted for far-reaching *constitutional amendments*, tabled on 31 July without prior consultation and amidst subsequent strong objections by other parties and a broad civil society alliance; these concerns were raised in a public statement on 21 August. The more than 40 amendments increased the number of seats by one-third from 72 to 96 in the next National Assembly to be elected. The same expansion by one-third was set for the National Council, based on the now 14 (originally 13) regions of the country. The appointment of regional governors by the head of state was also introduced as a constitutional clause. President Hifikepunye Lucas Pohamba had already been making such appointments, guided by an earlier law. This law and its implementation violated the original constitutional clause, which foresaw the election of governors by the other elected members of the regional councils. The amendments also consolidated *presidential control over state affairs* and added further power to an already strong executive president. The president now had the sole discretion to appoint or dismiss all heads of the state's security organs and was hence in exclusive control of all security agencies. Namibia's de facto one-party democracy thereby moved as from the next legislative period even closer to a one-person democracy, depending upon the degree to which the office holder was willing to use – or abuse – the presidential powers.

SWAPO's *electoral college* took place on 30–31 August. Delegates voted for the party list for the elections on the basis of the 'zebra style regulation' adopted by an extraordinary party congress in 2013. It had decided that every second candidate on the list (after the seated party leadership, ranking highest by virtue of their offices) had to be female. This was also considered to have been the ultimate reason for the earlier decision to increase the number of seats in the National Assembly – to avoid too many of the old male comrades falling by the wayside. Despite this cautious initiative, the election result came as a total surprise and was dubbed a 'tsunami' by some media. Among those who did not make it onto the total list of 96 candidates were four ministers, five deputy ministers and the speaker, as well as some other MPs. Accusations of 'de-campaigning', which accused party internal factions of having mobilised against certain candidates, thereby violating party rules, caused unrest and tensions. While the party's secretary-general announced an investigation into the allegations, it was also confirmed that the list remained valid. According to the constitutional amendments adopted, the next state president would be entitled to nominate in total eight additional MPs without voting rights; they would also be entitled to cabinet appointments. As a result, speculation continued for the rest of the year as to who would be offered access to political office by the new elected president before the swearing in of the next parliament. On 28 November, close to 900,000 Namibians (72% of a registered electorate of more than 1.2 m, out of a total estimated population of 2.3 m) voted in the country's fifth *parliamentary and presidential elections* since Independence. The use of electronic voting machines resulted in an embarrassing logistical and technological disaster. Thousands of voters were reportedly unable to participate in the elections due to various hiccups, despite often queuing for most of Election Day, if not longer (some polling stations remained open until the next morning while voters waited through the night). Even with extended opening, an undisclosed number of Namibians were denied their fundamental right to make a choice. While this had no serious impact on the results, it threw a shadow on their democratic integrity.

The result was predictable, though the extent of *SWAPO's overwhelming dominance* surprised most observers. While the former liberation movement had secured well above a two-thirds majority in every election since 1994, the party this time crossed the 80% mark and took 77 seats in direct competition with 15 other parties. Nine opposition parties won a total of 19 of the 96 seats in the National Assembly for the next five-year legislative period, starting with Independence Day on 21 March 2015. The opposition was more divided than ever before, underlining the lack of meaningful political alternatives. Presidential candidate Hage Geingob topped the presidential vote with a whopping 86% against eight other contenders, scoring even higher than his predecessors Sam Nujoma and Hifikepunye Pohamba.

The signs of *democratic authoritarianism* suggested that, while the country fulfilled all the formal criteria for a democracy (multiparty state, regular elections, democratic constitutional principles, civil liberties and a fairly independent judiciary, combined with independent media and freedom of speech), there was not a level playing field. While observers testified to free and fair elections, the term 'fair' seemed to be relative. SWAPO was the only party that had the machinery and financial means (not least through massive donations from a private sector that benefitted from government and state business) to mobilise countrywide. Evidence of the unfair practices possible in such an environment included SWAPO's purchase of considerable time from the state owned Namibian Broadcasting Company (NBC) for the live televising of its final political star rally.

Notwithstanding these limitations and despite a new degree of social protest in both words and deeds, no meaningful credible social and political alternatives to SWAPO were in sight. On the contrary, the ruling party's approval ratings remained unchallenged. Findings of an *Afrobarometer* survey presented in March concluded that the "political system seems to deliver more democracy than the population seems to demand", while a participatory political culture had not yet been developed. While democratic consolidation might be a feature in the institutional domain, "democratic values, behaviours and expectations are yet to catch up". This did not prevent a comparatively good ranking in the Bertelsmann Stiftung's Transformation Index released early in the year, which placed Namibia in the overall status index at 30th out of 129 countries, and 25th in political transformation.

Foreign Affairs

A series of bilateral interactions with *African states* took place during the year. Nigerian President Goodluck Jonathan attended the Independence Day celebrations as part of a state visit on 20–21 March. President Pohamba attended Senegal's Independence Day ceremonies on 4 April as the guest of honour. Namibia announced that it would open an embassy there. Pohamba visited Swaziland on 14–17 May reciprocating a state visit by King Mswati III in 2013. Former head of state Sam Nujoma, as head of the AU observer mission, and Foreign Minister Netumbo Nandi-Ndaitwah, as head of the SADC Electoral Observer Mission, declared the *elections in Malawi* of 30 May "generally credible" and "peaceful, free, transparent and credible, reflecting the will of the people", respectively. During October, *South Africa* finally lived up to a promise made during a state visit by President Zuma in November 2013 to donate N\$ 100 m in support of the drought relief programme in Namibia.

The *look East* policy continued. While on a state visit to *China*, Prime Minister Geingob met President Xi Jinping on 8 April. He confirmed the will to create a favourable environment for closer collaboration with Chinese investors. Chinese business interests in

Namibia remained high and the number of Chinese locally resident remained a constant matter of speculation and provoked strong feelings among ordinary people. In December, a local newspaper claimed to have information that China had negotiated with the government to use the deep-sea port of Walvis Bay as a naval base. A delegation from *North Korea* headed by the deputy minister for trade made a visit on 15–17 May and explored further intensification of trade relations. The North Korean state construction company Mansudae Overseas Project Group of Companies, a subsidiary or alias of Korea Mining Development Trade Corporation (KOMID), had in the past 15 years won several major tenders for prominent public works, especially for national monuments and government offices. During the year, it was building an ammunition factory at the Luiperdsvalley military base outside Windhoek. KOMID was among the companies on the boycott list attached to the UNSC Resolution 1718 (2006). All business transactions with the listed companies were in violation of the resolution.

The long controversy around the EU-initiated *EPA* was finally brought to an end during negotiations in July, when the SADC group, in which Namibia was the most vocal advocate, reached a compromise on some of the most contentious issues (such as the elimination of subsidies on all products exported to Namibia, the right to export duties on some products, an infant industry protection strategy and non-compliance with the Most Favoured Nations clause). But while ratifying the adjusted agreement, Namibia continued to look for additional options to expand trade relations. After two years of negotiations, a trade cooperation treaty was signed with *Turkey* on 5 November.

UN Secretary-General (UNSG) *Ban Ki-moon* visited on 24–25 June for the official opening of the UN offices (already operational for seven years). He applauded the country for its democratic policy and the media freedom, as well as for its human rights record. President Pohamba complained that Namibia's classification as an upper-middle-income country would not reflect the huge income discrepancies inherited from colonialism and would negatively impact on efforts to reduce poverty. He also urged the UNSG to address UNSC reform, in order to make the UNSC more democratic and representative and to provide a permanent seat for an African nation. Pohamba's renewal of blame of Apartheid for the current skewed income provoked critical comments from the public. The minister of health and social services declared on behalf of Pohamba in a statement on 8 December that a decline in *donor health funding* had negatively impacted on Namibia's ability to deliver high-quality, effective and accessible health services.

Socioeconomic Developments

In February, the *IMF* published the 2013 Article IV Consultation, which applauded Namibia for "impressive strides in economic development" since Independence. But it also concluded that this had not resulted in sufficient job creation and lower inequality. A matter of special concern was the high cost of state-owned enterprises (SOEs) and the need "to put them on a financially viable footing".

Minister of Finance Saara Kuugongelwa-Amadhila tabled the *annual budget* for the fiscal year 2014/15 on 19 February. With an estimated expenditure of N\$ 60.3 bn it represented a 26.7% increase of N\$ 12.7 bn on the previous year and thereby the second largest growth in expenditure since Independence. This could be seen as a sign of investments in line with the election year. Staff costs rose from N\$ 17.5 bn to N\$ 22 bn (mainly for salaries in education and the military), representing 37% of total expenditure. Projected revenue increased by 25% to N\$ 52.5 bn, of which SACU revenue was estimated at N\$ 18.1 bn or 34.7% of total revenue. The minister in her budget speech admitted to "a significant risk" with regard to the "uncertainty regarding future SACU revenues due to on-going reforms". The budget deficit was projected at N\$ 7.6 bn or 5.4% of

GDP, to be covered mainly from domestic market borrowing. Total debt increased to about N$ 38.5 bn or 27.2% of GDP.

In terms of *sectoral allocations*, education again received the largest share with N$ 13.1 bn (22.7%). Defence was the second largest, with N$ 6.6 bn. Another N$ 6.1 bn was allocated to the health sector and N$ 6 bn to the Finance Ministry. The last included transfers of N$ 2.5 bn each to SOEs and foreign and domestic interest rate payments to cover growing debt services. The fiscal policy was nevertheless widely considered as relatively sound both by local economists and by international financial institutions and rating agencies. Once again, the budget that was presented, as well as the subsequent analyses and debates in the public sphere through local media, financial experts and think tanks, testified to a high degree of transparency and accountability in comparison with most other practices on the continent.

The election year left its mark with another N$ 8.3 bn put aside for regional and local government, housing and rural development, with a continued emphasis on the provision of low-cost *housing* throughout the country, for which a special mass housing scheme had been launched in 2013. Its implementation, however, left much room for improvement. Many cases were reported of tenders being awarded to newly created companies in Namibian ownership that had no specific competence except good connections to SWAPO's inner circle. After tenders were awarded, these local 'tenderpreneurs' often sub-contracted foreign companies and pocketed considerable portions of the money as brokers. Many of the projects were delayed, remained incomplete or were sub-standard, and criticism mounted. As a result, the government decided towards the end of May to put the N$ 2.9 bn mass housing project introduced in 2013 on hold. Similarly, the Targeted Intervention Programme for Employment and Economic Growth (*TIPEEG*) announced with much fanfare in 2012 and allocated a total of N$ 14.5 bn for the three-year period, had created by the time of the budget presentation over 15,000 permanent and over 67,000 temporary jobs – many fewer than originally promised. Critics bemoaned the fact that large amounts of the money under TIPEEG were wasted on intermediaries rather than being invested effectively in lasting employment creation, and that no coherent strategic plan existed for efficient investment.

Despite the continued high budget allocations to *education*, efficiency remained low. In January, the examination results for the school year that ended in December were released. Of about 42,000 higher secondary school leavers, only some 10,800 met the minimum admission criteria for university studies. According to the 'Global Information Technology Report 2014' released by the World Economic Forum in April, mathematics and science education in Namibian schools was deteriorating and it ranked Namibia 128th out of 148 countires. The overall quality of the education system was ranked 118th, while the 95% adult literacy rate compared favourably with many other countries on the continent. *Unemployment* remained at an estimated high 30% (widely considered a conservative figure), and much higher in the age group to 30 years, with more than half in that age group without employment. Similarly, *poverty*-related features affected more than half of the population and remained a challenge in a country ranked as a higher-middle-income country with an annual average per-capita income of some $ 6,000, while at the same time, according to the UNDP Human Development Report, having the highest Gini-coefficient (which measures the unequal distribution of wealth) of all countries.

Mining remained the backbone of the *economy*, with diamonds (off- and on-shore), zinc and lead mainly exploited in the southern regions, gold and copper concentrated in the central and northern parts and uranium in the Namib desert along the Atlantic coast Many international mining companies ran the operations, with a growing Chinese ownership mainly in the uranium sector. Fisheries and agriculture added to the central relevance of the primary sector, while tourism was another source of income. Manufacturing remained low but its share in GDP gradually increased.

Energy supply remained a bottleneck. Dependency on power supplied by South Africa's utility company Eskom came under threat due to shortages of power in South Africa itself. This required further plans to secure future access to new sources. In April, the national power utility NamPower announced plans to set up a N$ 3 bn solar hybrid power plant and a waste oil recycling plant at the mining town of Arandis some 50 km from the Atlantic coast. A further N$ 7 bn was announced to be invested in transmission expansion to ensure reliable delivery of electricity to all parts of the country over the next few years. Finally, the establishment of a N$ 3 bn 250 MW long-term generation facility was planned for the Erongo region.

The Namibia *2011 Census Mortality Report* was released by the National Statistics Agency on 29 July. It recorded 44 deaths for every 1,000 live births and 604 maternal deaths per 100,000 live births. Fertility rates remained at an average of 3.9 children – among the lowest in SSA. Death by accidents (1,613), suicide (673) and murder (472) contributed to the overall recorded causes of mortality amounting to around 22,668 registered deaths, mainly due to illness. Life expectancy stood at 53 years for men and 60 years for women. Suicide rates were markedly higher than the world average and ranked among the highest in the world in the northern region, while traffic-related deaths were proportionally the highest worldwide. *HIV prevalence* had gradually declined in recent years but remained high. A 2014 Surveillance Report presented at the end of December showed a fall in the percentage of pregnant women who were HIV-positive from 18.2% in 2012 to 16.9%. But as the minister of health and social services concluded, the overall sustained high prevalence implied a need for continued expansion of antiretroviral treatment services. A long legal battle over the forced *sterilisation of HIV-positive women* in public hospitals was brought to an end by a final verdict of the Supreme Court on 3 November, when it ruled that the rights of three claimants had been violated by forced sterilisation, a practice documented since 2007. Despite a slight decline in mainly AIDS-related *tuberculosis* cases to just below 10,000 during the year, Namibia ranked according to WHO figures as the fourth-worst TB affected country in the world.

An *Afrobarometer* survey published in March pointed to a "strong perception among Namibians that inequality and unemployment are the key problems that Namibian democracy needs to address". In a subsequent survey, summarised on 18 November, 78% of the respondents favoured the adoption of a Basic Income Grant; more than 80% wanted a reform of the tender system to "eliminate nepotism and favouritism"; 86% criticised the emphasis on party loyalty and its reward system by means of 'jobs for the boys'; and 87% objected to further salary increases for political office bearers and executives in SOEs.

At the end of the year, many international media ranked Namibia among the world's most attractive tourist destinations. This accentuated the contrasts between rich and poor in this 'land of wide open spaces', where much room for improvement remained.

Namibia in 2015

The year saw the ascendancy of the new Head of State Hage
Geingob, perhaps the last member of the first generation of the
former liberation movement SWAPO (South West Africa People's
Organisation). He took over from Hifikepunye Pohamba, who was
for his two terms in office awarded the Mo Ibrahim Prize for good
governance. Geingob introduced several institutional innovations
and expanded the senior level of the administration. This increased
government expenditure and added to the growing fiscal stress. The
economic fragility was also exacerbated by global economic volatility and other negative factors. Despite the limitations of the promised prosperity under Geingob, SWAPO further extended its political
hegemony through regional and local elections in November. With
hardly any opposition remaining in both national chambers and on
regional and local authority levels, Namibian democracy de facto
was dependent on one party. In terms of its foreign policy, Namibia
clearly continued to turn more to the East and announced its
planned withdrawal from the ICC.

Domestic Politics

President-elect Hage Geingob had already taken several initiatives
before his swearing in on 21 March. On 2 February, a *presidential
council* was announced, composed of Geingob and his two predecessors, the previous prime ministers and their deputies. Nickey
Iyambo was appointed as Namibia's first vice president. He had
served in all cabinets over the previous 25 years and was the lon-
gest-serving minister of the first generation of post-Independence
politicians. Among the eight additional MPs appointed with non-
voting rights by the president were Pendukeni Iivula-Ithana and
Jerry Ekandjo, the two internal party nominees for president who

© KONINKLIJKE BRILL NV, LEIDEN, 2016 | DOI 10.1163/9789004321571_014

had lost to Geingob. He also resuscitated the fading political careers of Minister of Presidential Affairs Albert Kawana and Governor of the Hardap region Katrina Hanse-Himarwa as members of 'Team Hage'. The former deputy speaker and retired bishop Zephania Kameeta, also from the party's old guard, was brought back to take specific responsibility for the newly created portfolio of poverty eradication and social welfare. The *new cabinet* was announced on 19 March. Four new ministries were created and seven portfolios were renamed. The top-heavy executive structure seemed to represent an effort to reconcile internal party divisions and to secure loyalty. In particular, the expansion of the second-tier level of deputy ministers from 18 to 32 was most likely aimed at inclusivity. Added to the 28 cabinet members, this meant that almost 60% of all MPs were top government officials and led to an estimated 30% increase in the cost of government from N\$ 50 m under the Pohamba administration to N\$ 65 m. This generosity was widely considered a strategic investment in internal party stability to anchor Geingob's office as president in structures that create loyalty among the beneficiaries. Geingob also recruited several high-paid advisors to the Office of the President, whom he originally called the 'A-team', leaving the media and wider public wondering what role the ministers were supposed to play.

Amidst controversies as to the procedure and in a reportedly tense atmosphere, retired head of state Hifikepunye Pohamba in a surprise move handed over the *party presidency* to Geingob at a SWAPO central committee meeting on 18 April – well ahead of the scheduled elections at the next party congress in 2017. The politburo rejected Geingob's proposal that he be replaced as the party's vice president by a trusted office holder, and so he now held both party offices and the state presidency, which gave him a strong advantage over potential contenders for the next round of leadership contests in both the party and the state.

The president's first *State of the Nation Address*, given in parliament on 21 April showed a clear shift in language from the hitherto mainly party-dominated patriotic history, which had cultivated an exclusive narrative of SWAPO as the sole liberator. Geingob presented a more inclusive discourse. SWAPO was not mentioned once. Instead, the *Namibian house* was created as the new figurative core image and reference point and this metaphor continued to be a constant and integral feature of the president's public statements. However, while deliberately stressing the inclusivity of the nation-building project, Geingob promoted exclusionary tendencies by refusing to comment on gay rights. He also confirmed that those who had fought on the side of the South African army against SWAPO would not be eligible for war veteran status or for the pension awarded to those who had fought for SWAPO. Neither did the president show any inclination towards reconciliation with activists of the party's *Youth League*, four of whom (including the president) had been suspended the year before. They were finally expelled, reportedly at Geingob's instigation, at a meeting of the party's central committee, on 23 July. In August, they announced that they were starting legal proceedings against what they considered a violation of internal party disciplinary procedures.

Reconciliation did take place on other fronts, however. The former foreign minister, Hidipo Hamutenya, who had fallen out with the party leadership in 2004 in the battle for the country's presidency, had then established the Rally for Democracy and Progress (RDP) as an opposition party. After initial successes as the official opposition, it had faltered and become irrelevant. Hamutenya returned to SWAPO on 28 August and other previously higher-ranking SWAPO members who had joined him in the RDP followed his lead. At a SWAPO gathering on 21 November, Hamutenya urged the party to rally behind President Geingob. The collapse of the RDP was widely considered as another sign that the *SWAPO hegemony* was becoming further entrenched, with the cooptation of several leading opposition members.

In a surprise move, Geingob appointed Katuutire Kaura, the former president of the Democratic Turnhalle Alliance (DTA), on

25 September as advisor to the governor of the Kunene region – the only region in which SWAPO held no absolute majority until the forthcoming *regional council and local authority elections* on 27 November. The media expressed great concern that the opposition parties seemed weaker than ever and that election campaigns were largely absent. The only newsworthy items were internal SWAPO power struggles over the list of candidates: 26 of the 121 regional council constituencies and five of the 57 local authorities were left uncontested to SWAPO, which showed the organisational weakness of the opposition. Voter turnout for the 95 contested constituencies in the regional elections was 36.5%, an all-time low. SWAPO candidates took 112 elected regional council seats and won a clear majority in all 14 regions. All but two of the 42 members of the National Council were SWAPO representatives and SWAPO remained in firm control of 54 of the 57 local authorities. For many observers, this was a clear indication that there was not much democratic competition left in Namibia.

The *high treason trial* over the failed attempt at secession in the Eastern Caprivi region of 2 August 1999 finally ended with a verdict on 8 December. Of the originally more than 120 accused, around 30 were found guilty and received long jail sentences. More than 20 of those originally arrested had died in jail (bail was refused even for those suffering from serious medical conditions), while most others had their charges dismissed during the course of the trial. Many of them had spent up to 16 years in prison. The judge harshly criticised the police for using torture to force those arrested to implicate others and to confess.

On 20 November, retired president Pohamba received the 2014 *Mo Ibrahim Prize* for African Leadership in Accra for his terms in office. The prize, given to heads of state in recognition of good governance, had not been awarded to anyone for several years. The media and the wider public applauded the recognition, despite having been rather critical of Pohamba in the past.

Foreign Affairs

Despite his appeal to cabinet members to limit their travel activities, President Geingob was absent from Namibia on a number of occasions during his first nine months in office. The *intensive presidential travel schedule* included visits to 19 cities in 14 countries. A working trip to Angola on 16 April was Geingob's first state visit. On 20 April, he attended the SADC Summit in Harare (Zimbabwe), followed by a working visit to South Africa where he met president Jacob Zuma on 6 May. On 29 May, he attended the inauguration of President Buhari in Nigeria and visited Mali, and on 10 June he was a co-signatory to the Sharm-el-Sheikh declaration launching the COMESA-EAC-SADC Tripartite Free Trade Agreement in Egypt. He made a state visit to Cuba on 14–16 September before visiting the USA to receive the African Political Leader Award on 18 September in Washington DC (jointly with the Gambian autocrat Jammeh) and an Honorary Doctorate at Fordham University in New York on 22 September, to deliver his maiden speech at the opening of the 70th UN General Assembly and to receive the Africa-America Institute Lifetime Achievements and Distinguished Alumnus Award, both on 29 September. He made an official state visit to Tanzania on 11–12 October, and attended the 3rd Africa-India Forum Summit in New Delhi at the end of October. On 27 November, Geingob left for a three-day general meeting of the Commonwealth Heads of State in Malta, followed by attendance at the COP 21 climate summit in Paris on 31 November and participation in a Global Africa Investment Summit in London on 1–2 December. The tour concluded with the China-Africa-Forum in Johannesburg (South Africa) on 4–5 December. The local newspaper 'The Namibian' reported on 18 December that, according to its own investigations, the president had earned an additional N\$ 2.4 m in travel allowances during the year, and had flown more than 70,000 km at a minimum cost of N\$ 3.5 m in airplane fuel.

For the *AU Summit* in Johannesburg on 14 June, Geingob had prepared a speech in which he praised Robert Mugabe as his role model and lashed out against the *ICC* as an abomination because of its undue interference in the internal affairs of sovereign states. During his state visit to Tanzania on 11–12 October, he lobbied for the withdrawal of Tanzania from the ICC. In line with recommendations already formulated earlier by the African National Congress in South Africa and SWAPO at home, Minister of Information and government spokesman Tjekero Tweya announced at a press conference on 23 November that the government had decided to withdraw from the ICC as part of a reformulation of the country's foreign policy.

On 15 June, the foreign ministers of Namibia and *South Africa* signed an MoU concerning the allocation of a pledge made on the occasion of an earlier state visit by President Zuma in November 2013 for 100 m South African rand in drought relief, half to be spent on procurement of seeds and maize meal and half on drilling boreholes and related water projects. In a rare sign of international solidarity by members of the public, some 200 mainly younger people had demonstrated on 28 April against xenophobic attacks taking place in South Africa, and had marched on the South African High Commission in the Namibian capital, Windhoek, and handed over a petition, asserting that violence against any African was an attack on all Africans.

Friendly relations with *China*, officially termed an 'all-weather friendship', continued. On 30 March, a top-ranking Chinese military delegation led by State Councillor and Defence Minister Chang Wanquan met President Geingob in Windhoek, thereby reinforcing earlier rumours that the Chinese government intended to establish a naval base in Walvis Bay harbour. Questioned at a press conference the next day, Geingob mentioned that rumours might kill a country. Confronted with speculation during the BBC's 'Hard Talk' on 1 December, Geingob neither confirmed nor denied

Chinese interest in the naval base. The US Embassy in Windhoek on 10 December categorically denied that the USA had approached the government with a view to obtaining a naval base in Walvis Bay, contrary to what Geingob had indicated during the 'Hard Talk' interview. Attending the China-Africa Forum Summit in Johannesburg on 4/5 December, Geingob met again with Chinese President Xi Jinping, whom he had already visited in 2014 when he had been prime minister. In his speech there, he emphasised that the partnership with China "is one built on long lasting and historic solidarity, as well as mutual respect. It is therefore offensive when we are lectured by certain nations and warned about the so-called Chinese colonization of Africa." He applauded a number of key Chinese investments in Namibia and praised as invaluable the two countries' deepening cooperation, especially with regard to infrastructure. Chinese companies had huge stakes in Namibian nuclear mining operations and were in control of large parts of the construction industry, dominating competition for public tenders in the sector such as for roads, railways, harbours, airports and office buildings.

Diplomatic relations with *Western countries* featured less prominently. French Minister for Ecology, Sustainable Development and Energy Ségolène Royal visited Namibia in early August and met with the president and her counterparts at the Ministry for Mines and Energy. The French mining giant Areva was among the major companies with operations in Namibia's uranium sector. Accusations of graft and a probe into dubious deals, which involved Geingob as a former Areva consultant, emerged in early December. Neither the company nor the president commented on their past relationship.

Relations with *Germany* were historically close but also precarious. During the year, both countries entered a new stage as the German government indicated that it was prepared to accept the term genocide as appropriate description of the atrocities committed against the anti-colonial resistance movement (1904–1907).

At the end of the year, both countries appointed special representatives in order to seek a common ground with regard to dealing with their shared past. Meanwhile, representatives of German civil society and agencies of the descendants of the Namibian victim groups complained that they were not part of the negotiations.

Socioeconomic Developments

Overall, public concern over the government's economic policy and its expenditure rose considerably during the first months of the Geingob administration, and was also fuelled by the marked increase in the number of highly-paid senior officials and the expansion of the cabinet, alongside considerably increased benefits for political office bearers.

Average annual per capita income of $ 9,418 for the estimated population of 2.3 m put Namibia into the category of a higher middle-income country. According to the 2014 data presented in UNDP's Human Development Report (HDR) for 2015, it ranked along with Morocco as 126th out of 188 countries on the HDI index, with a value of 0.628, placing it in the *medium human development category*. But when the HDI is adjusted for inequality, it falls by 43.6% to 0.354, leading to a drop of 25 places (the second worst world-wide after Iran). On the basis of 2013 data, the HDR categorised 44.9% of the population as living in *multiple poverty* – 21.4% higher than the proportion of people living on a daily income of less than $ 1.25 and hence classified as 'extremely poor' on the basis of their monetary income. 'Multiple poverty', on the other hand, is a category that considers access to health and education facilities, sanitation, water and related services as factors contributing to destitution. A further 19.3% of the population were classified as close to multiple poverty. This means that almost two-thirds of the population were living in multiple poverty. Average life expectancy was 64.8 years (62 for men and 67.3 for women). This represented a gradual increase in life expectancy, returning to figures at Independence, and suggested that the worst effects of HIV/AIDS, with the accompanying decline of life expectancy, had been left behind.

New Minister of Finance Calle Schlettwein presented the annual *budgets* 2015/16 to 2017/18 on 31 March. Four key priorities were identified for guiding fiscal policy: inclusive growth, poverty reduction, wealth creation and service delivery, including accountability and value for money. For the year 2015/16, a revenue increase of 11.4% was forecast (N$ 58.4 bn). Expenditure was expected to increase by 11.6% to N$ 67.1 bn, of which 83.5% was allocated as an operational budget and 16.5% as a development budget for investment. Close to N$ 4 bn were earmarked as interest payments for debt servicing. Voting on expenditure again allocated the highest proportion to the two educational ministries, which received in total almost N$ 15 bn. The Ministry of Defence was, as in previous years, the second largest recipient of funds with N$ 7.2 bn, followed by the health ministry with N$ 6.5 bn and the police with N$ 4.7 bn. The policy of subsidies for state-owned enterprises continued unabated with transfers of approximately 14% of total spending, mainly to support operational activities. Investments from the development budget were mainly allocated to transport (N$ 2.8 bn), urban and rural development (N$ 1.3 bn) and agriculture, water and forestry (N$ 1.2 bn).

The ongoing *deficit* contributed to a further rise in the debt-to-GDP ratio, which was expected to double despite a major increase in GDP from the 2011 level of 16% to well above 30%. As observed in an analysis carried out by the local Institute for Public Policy Research (IPPR), "this trend is highly concerning and ultimately not sustainable". Total government guarantees were projected to increase to 11.3% of GDP by 2017/18, well beyond the original target of 10% maximum. As the IPPR commented, this highlighted the government's "continued utilization of all possible funding sources, to their maximum". Figures produced by the Bank of Namibia showed that at the end of November state *debt* had increased by 21% from N$ 32.2 bn in 2014 to N$ 39 bn, while foreign currency reserves were close to N$ 23.8 bn, compared with N$ 22.7 bn a year before. In October, the government raised a second Eurobond of US$ 750 m (equivalent to some N$ 10.4 bn at the exchange rate then), of which US$ 300 m would be used to support the foreign reserve position and US$ 450 m to finance development projects. By year's end, estimates suggested that, due to the additional borrowing, a lower than expected GDP growth and the unfavourable currency exchange rate (the N$ is pegged to the South African rand, which during the year depreciated by over 30%) debt had accumulated to account for over 35% of GDP, which government had originally declared the maximum ceiling for its fiscal policy. Financial observers expressed growing concern at the lack of fiscal prudence. In a press release on 24 September, the IMF summarised the Article IV Consultation and warned that, due to several factors, risks to a sound economy were increasing. Meanwhile, the trade deficit increased by over 100% in the third quarter of the year compared with 2014, and displayed vulnerability to external shocks.

On 3 November, Finance Minister Schlettwein presented a *mid-year budget review* to parliament and had bad news as regards the income from the SACU revenue fund, which had run an estimated deficit of N$ 7.6 bn in the 2014/15 financial year. This implied not only a downward adjustment of future SACU receipts (which account for a third of Namibia's total revenue), but also repayment of a N$ 3 bn share for the next financial year. He also announced a downward adjustment of 4.9% in revenue income to N$ 55.6 bn and necessary cost-saving measures to reduce expenditure, as well as re-allocation of funds between ministries to meet spending priorities. Meanwhile, salary increases for civil servants were also announced to the tune of N$ 1 bn, while criticism of a highly paid bloated public service (with some 100,000 employees) grew. The proposed introduction of a 'solidarity tax', originally applicable to monthly incomes over N$ 6,600 was heavily criticised by the public, who felt that first those better and best off should be taxed at a higher rate. Government then backtracked and announced that the idea would be thought through again – an indication that certain concerns were still under consideration by policy makers.

Soon after moving into office, president Geingob had announced an increase in the old-age pension for those over 60 years of age from N$ 600 to N$ 1,000 a month as a much welcome effort to reduce poverty. He also created a new ministry for poverty alleviation and declared the fight against poverty to be his government's top priority, but little was achieved during the year to ease the general misery, and *hunger* remained a daily experience for many ordinary Namibians. According to information presented at a Food and Nutrition Security strategic review workshop in early September, the UN State of Food Insecurity Report for 2015 showed that 42.3% of the population was undernourished in 2014, compared with 27.3% in 2002. These data contrasted with claims that poverty had been reduced by 11% during the previous decade. On 20 November, the local UNICEF representative announced that an estimated 270,000 children were living in poverty, with 140,000 of them in severe circumstances. A total of 880,000 Namibians (42%) were below the age of 18, while the same percentage of Namibians was classified by FAO as malnourished.

The *school system* continued to perform dismally. After some positive trends in 2014, the end of year exams showed a decline in pass rates at senior school level. Grade 12 (school leaving) exams were passed by 6,056 students with results that allow access to university, i.e. about one-fifth fewer than in the previous year (7,536). Pass rates in the grade 10 exams required for access to senior school levels, were only obtained by some 20,000 out of 37,000 students (about 54%). Insufficiently trained and under-motivated teachers, lack of material infrastructure, and the unsupportive environment provided by the living conditions of many students were considered as contributing factors, as well as the inefficient spending of state funds.

Strong El Nino effects led to a massive *drought*. The municipality of Windhoek announced water restrictions in the capital towards the end of the year after several appeals to reduce household consumption showed little result. Water reserves fell dramatically and an emergency was looming. The situation in rural areas, which had suffered already from bad harvests in 2014, continued to deteriorate. An Agricultural Inputs and Household Food Security Situation report released in December by the National Early Warning and Food Information Unit warned that household *food security* had significantly weakened in the seven major northern communal crop-producing regions, as most households had exhausted their supplies from the poor harvest of the last season. Food insecurity was exacerbated by the fact that a large number of draught animals that were used to plough had died because of the drought. A hefty price increase for stable foods was predicted, which would further worsen the situation.

Natural resources were depleted not only with respect to extensive land use, underground minerals and fish along the coast, but also by *poaching*, which increased dramatically. By the end of the year a total of at least 80 rhinos had been killed illegally (mainly in the Etosha National Park), compared with the 25 registered in 2014, four in 2013 and two in 2012. A spectacular on-going court case implicated four Chinese citizens in smuggling rhino horns and other illegal hunting trophies and there were allegations that high-ranking officials were also involved in such organised crime. The Chinese-Namibian friendship seemed to be effective in multiple aspects, though growing sentiment among ordinary people seemed to suggest it was not welcomed by all.

Further Reading

The following monographs and edited volumes published since 2000 offer background information and analyses for those interested in more aspects of Namibian society.

Becker, Barbara, *Speaking Out: Namibians Share Their Perspectives On Independence*. Windhoek: Out of Africa 2005

Bösl, Anton, André du Pisani and Dennis U. Zaire (eds), *Namibia's Foreign Relations. Historic contexts, current dimensions, and perspectives for the 21st Century*. Windhoek: MacMillan Education and Konrad Adenauer Foundation 2014

Bösl, Anton, Nico Horn and André du Pisani (eds), *Constitutional Democracy in Namibia. A Critical Analysis After Two Decades*. Windhoek: MacMillan Education and Konrad Adenauer Foundation 2010

Diener, Ingolf and Olivier Grafe (eds), *Contemporary Namibia. The First Landmarks of a Post-Apartheid Society*. Windhoek: Gamsberg MacMillan 2001

Du Pisani, André, Reinhart Kössler and William A. Lindeke (eds), *The Long Aftermath of War – Reconciliation and Transition in Namibia*. Freiburg: Arnold Bergstraesser Institut 2010

Friedman, John T., *Imagining the Post-Apartheid State. An Ethnographic Account of Namibia*. New York and Oxford: Berghahn 2011

Horn, Nico and Anton Bösl (eds), *Human Rights and the Rule of Law in Namibia*. Windhoek: MacMillan Namibia 2008

Jauch, Herbert, Lucy Edwards and Braam Cupido, *A Rich Country With Poor People: Inequality in Namibia*. Windhoek: Labour Resource and Research Institute 2009

Keulder, Christiaan (ed.), *State, Society and Democracy. A Reader in Namibian Politics*. Windhoek: MacMillan Education and Konrad Adenauer Foundation 2010 (reprint; originally 2000)

Kössler, Reinhart, *Namibia and Germany. Negotiating the Past*. Windhoek: UNAM Press and Münster: Westfälisches Dampfboot 2015

Leys, Colin and Susan Brown, *Histories of Namibia: Living through the liberation struggle*. London: Merlin Press 2005

Melber, Henning, *Understanding Namibia. The trials of independence*. London: Hurst and Auckland Park: Jacana 2014 and New York: Oxford University Press 2015

Melber, Henning (ed.), *Re-examining Liberation in Namibia: Political Culture Since Independence*. Uppsala: Nordic Africa Institute 2003

Melber, Henning (ed.), *Transitions in Namibia: Which Changes for Whom?* Uppsala: Nordic Africa Institute 2007

Sherbourne, Robin, *Guide to the Namibian Economy 2013/14*. Windhoek: Institute for Public Policy Research 2013

Silvester, Jeremy (ed.), *Re-Viewing Resistance in Namibian History.* Windhoek: UNAM Press 2015

Southall, Roger, *Liberation Movements in Power: Party and State in Southern Africa*. Woodbridge: James Currey and Scottsville: UKZN Press 2013

Tötemeyer, Gerhard, *Church and State in Namibia. The Politics of Reconciliation*. Freiburg: Arnold Bergstraesser Institut 2010

Tvedten, Inge, *'As long as they don't bury me here': Social relations of poverty in a Namibian shanty town*. Basel: Basler Afrika Bibliographien 2011

Von Wietersheim, Erika, *This land is my land! Motions and emotions around land reform in Namibia*. Windhoek: Friedrich Ebert Foundation 2008

Wallace, Marion, with John Kinahan, *A History of Namibia: From the Beginning to 1990*. London: Hurst 2011

Winterfeldt, Volker, Tom Fox and Pempelani Mufune (eds), *Namibia – Society – Sociology*. Windhoek: University of Namibia Press 2002

Index

Printed in the United States
By Bookmasters